FINDING THE NARROW WAY

(A Spiritual Experience)

Michael A. Blomberg

WestBow
PRESS
A DIVISION OF THOMAS NELSON

WestBow Press books may be ordered through booksellers or by contacting:

WestBow Press
A Division of Thomas Nelson
1663 Liberty Drive
Bloomington, IN 47403
www.westbowpress.com
1-(866) 928-1240

ISBN: 978-1-4497-3609-5 (sc)
ISBN: 978-1-4497-3610-1 (hc)
ISBN: 978-1-4497-3608-8 (e)

Library of Congress Control Number: 2011963390

Printed in the United States of America

WestBow Press rev. date: 02/27/2012

The Lord gave the word; great was the company
of those who proclaimed it.
(Psalm 68:11)

Contents

Acknowledgments

I would like to humbly acknowledge my fiancée, Stephanie, for all of her support throughout my journey, and for always being there for me. I would like to thank my mother, Maureen, for her unconditional love and support, and my father, Bruce, for all of the positive guidance and words of wisdom he has shared with me throughout the years. I would like to thank all of the coaches, namely Steve Hayden and Frank Carey, for the valuable life lessons they have taught me through athletics. I would also wish to acknowledge spiritual authors Don Miguel Ruiz, Dr. David Jeremiah, Rabbi Jonathan Sacks, Rhonda Byrne, Beth Moore, and all of the ones who have come before me and who understand and live in truth. I would also like to thank the staff at WestBow Press for making the publishing of this book possible. Most importantly, I would like to thank God Almighty, the Spirit of the universe, because if it were not for His love and forgiveness, I would not be alive to write this book, and it is through His grace that I am able to share this with you.

Introduction

Greetings, dear reader; I would like to welcome you to my experience. I am writing this in hopes of sharing the good news in faith. I have much to share with you, but first I shall begin by giving you some background information about my life and my journey of faith. I would like to humbly thank you in advance, dear reader, and I hope that once you have finished reading, you will have gained a sense of enlightenment and clarity on how the world works.

To begin, my name is Michael and I was born at Salem Hospital in February, 1984, and I grew up on King Street, in the little town of Groveland, Massachusetts in the house that my dad built. I am a person who has always appreciated his life, his family, friends, and loved ones. Throughout my life, I had a curiosity as to what the meaning of life is. I used to contemplate the path of right living but evidently I needed some guidance to understand how I could find this very narrow path. As I take you through an in-depth spiritual journey, it is my hope that you may find answers to life's questions that you may have.

Life is a journey in and of itself. It can be a wonderful journey with joy, love, and laughter. The decisions of the individual will dictate where life takes a person. My journey has been very interesting, to say the least. Some ups and downs had gone on throughout my life until I woke up and realized I had been living my own personal dream. Since having that realization, I have been able to make positive changes and positive decisions. The days of peaks and valleys are behind me, and I am finally able to enjoy a more peaceful, smoother course on the sea of life. It is through the grace of a loving Creator, self-inquiry, and the teachings of spiritual authors that I have been able to make so many positive life changes. I have yet to meet any of these authors in person, and it is my hope that someday I will be able to do so in order to personally thank them for all of the wisdom they have provided me through their works, and for how they have helped me more than they will ever know.

As I grew spiritually along my journey, I really began to understand the teachings of the most spiritual human being who has ever walked God's green earth: Jesus of Nazareth. The teachings of Jesus are so simple, and yet hold so many answers to questions I've had and life situations I've been through. I found myself wondering why I hadn't read this earlier in life. I suppose there is a time and place for everything, and I believe that if I had read His teachings earlier, I would not have understood Him, because I did not have the eyes to see what I was reading. I shall include some of His teachings, as well as other pieces of Scripture in this book; however, I shall do my best to mention how these teachings match up with certain real-life experiences I have had. I have also realized that when a spiritual author writes a book, he or she is sending a positive message to the world in hopes to bring regular people, such as myself, into the Light. As I look into my past, I understand now that I am really living in life, whereas for a number of years I merely existed on earth. It took a degree of self-honesty for me to make the initial change, but the results have been electric. I have tried to share my message wherever I go; however, I have noticed that as human beings, we sometimes have a difficult time listening. We hear, but we don't listen. The difference between hearing and listening is as follows:

Hearing is a natural process, a physiological one (one of our physical senses as human beings). Everybody can "hear" (except those who are deaf), but not everybody can *truly listen* until they *learn* how.

Listening is a skill in which we try to understand the *true message* and the emotions behind the words, instead of just the facts.

In my experience, if I read about something that makes sense to me and I can relate it to my life, I will have a much easier time listening to others who have had similar experiences, because I am able to identify with what that person is saying. As I look back on my life, I realize that for a long time I did not understand myself completely, and I needed to know myself before I could honestly begin to listen to and understand others. In the beginning of my spiritual journey, I sought guidance from men and women who had been in my situation before. I'll use this analogy: as a quarterback, I did not need an offensive lineman to teach me how to throw a football. I needed an experienced quarterback to teach me how, someone who had lived it, someone who had been there before.

I have noticed in life that some of the most valuable lessons have cost me no money at all. Paying attention was all I had to do, and it is nice to finally be at peace with the world and the people around me. I shall briefly touch upon the difference between *faith* and *religion* (as I understand it). I will begin with my spiritual journey of faith, but I may include some flashbacks from time to time, so I shall make sure to add dates so as not to confuse you, the reader. I would like to also note that some of the names of people in my book have been changed to maintain anonymity. Also, the twelve-step program I have followed is an anonymous program, so I cannot mention the specific name, but I have created and included my own as outlined in chapter 3 to give you, the reader, an understanding.

CHAPTER ONE

The Program

My journey began on Sunday, August 15, 2010. I had entered a two-week program after pleading guilty to operating a motor vehicle under the influence of alcohol. Prior to checking in with the program, I purchased a couple of books to read during my free time. The first, *The Four Agreements*[1] by Don Miguel Ruiz had been recommended by Ron Cohen, a very nice older man whom I had met the previous year while working out at a local health club. As I look back, I can see that Ron was clearly a man who had had a thorough spiritual awakening. I selected the other book, *What in the World Is Going On?*[2] by Dr. David Jeremiah, at random.

While I wasn't overly happy to be away from home and the comforts thereof, I felt that I might as well learn as much as I could from the program. I began praying each night, asking God to help me to keep an open mind. I wanted to make the most out of the two weeks and learn as much as possible from the counselors. I also asked Him to bless my friends and my family, because I knew my family had been worried about me.

Wanting to utilize the time there, I paid attention when the counselors taught and read the handouts they provided. During the first three days of the program, I read *The Four Agreements*. The agreements mentioned are as follows:

1. *Be Impeccable with Your Word.* Ruiz mentions speaking truthfully with love and integrity. Avoiding gossip and not putting oneself down.
2. *Don't Take Anything Personally.* Ruiz mentions how what others say and do is a projection of their own reality, their own dream. He teaches how to become immune to the opinions and actions of others so as to avoid unnecessary suffering in life.
3. *Don't Make Assumptions.* Ruiz mentions finding the courage to ask questions and expressing what you really want and being a clear communicator to avoid drama and misunderstandings. This agreement is life changing in and of itself.
4. *Always Do Your Best.* Ruiz mentions how one's best may change from moment to moment, however simply doing one's best will help to avoid self-judgment, regret, and self-abuse, and lead to a more enjoyable life.

The Four Agreements was a life-changing book, and I would highly recommend it to anybody. It was obviously written by a man who has been completely saturated with the Spirit, a very wise and divine being. I realized that I was already following these agreements in my life to some extent, but if I continued to abuse alcohol and other chemical substances, I was going to drive myself insane "trying to be a better person." I thought that perhaps if I eliminated the use of chemicals in my life that I could become more like the author, Don Miguel Ruiz. This was a good mental wake-up call for me, but I wasn't sure how to go about it all, so I continued praying at night, listening, and paying attention to the counselors.

My ears seemed to open a little more each day, and I began to understand that the people (counselors and speakers) in this program were not preaching to me; they were trying to teach me based on their own life experiences. I listened in the nightly meetings, and I began to empathize with the speakers. It seemed as if I was feeling what they were feeling. I almost cried at times, but had to stop myself out of fear of embarrassment. I became more and more interested in the simple twelve-step program that they were teaching us about. The program's positive message of hope made me want to follow it. There were many required homework assignments I had to complete during this program. These assignments included recording daily reflections on what we were learning and how we felt.

One nightly meeting that stands out in my memory was on Sunday, August 22. After the speakers finished, I went up to thank them for sharing, and one (a woman about my mother's age) asked me how old I was. When I told her I was twenty-six, she commented, "You're so young." My first thought was, *what better time than now to start making some positive life changes.* This realization bore fruit in the days ahead.

Halfway through the program, we were required to write out timelines based on our life experiences with chemical substances, etc. I was very thorough with mine, and a lot of things that I hadn't thought about in years started to come back to me. It felt good to be honest with myself and to put those memories in writing.

I will never forget August 24, the Tuesday during the second week of the two-week program. During the morning group, we read our timelines. I volunteered to read mine first. As I read, I began to feel better. The last bullet on the timeline was where I was at that moment. I had written, *I am currently at a two-week program and I have made the decision to stop using alcohol and mind-altering substances because I am tired of wasting so much time and so much of my life.* I never would have thought that I would say or even think something like that, but I guess I needed some time and some quality information to come to the point of making that decision.

During the nightly meeting, a group of young men came in to speak. This was great for me, because these men were closer to my age than any of the previous groups that we had heard. They all mentioned how they used to lie, cheat, and steal while under the influence of mind-altering chemicals.

It was eye opening to see so much honesty from people in my age range, and it really hit home with me. I could relate to these men, and I was grateful to have the opportunity to hear them share their message of hope.

Later that night while I was praying, I said, "Thank You, Father; I understand now that throughout my trial period and through this entire situation that You have been teaching me." The minute I said this, I felt a warm presence, almost like a warm chill, flow through my body, and I began to cry. My tears were not tears of sadness, but tears of joy and gratitude because I was grateful that I never stopped praying and never stopped believing in God. Many so-called friends had said, "There is no God." Well, whatever proof I required had just been revealed to me. I was grateful that, even though there were many atheists in this program (I didn't even know about atheism prior to this time), it didn't hinder me from my faith and prayers. This, dear reader, is known as a *spiritual awakening.*

After this awakening, and while I was still crying, I had a revelation (an epiphany). I realized that the brunt of the problems in my life were a direct result of alcohol and mind-altering chemical abuse. I thought, *Wow! My life is pretty good! Imagine the possibilities if I just make the decision to stop now. Maybe this all happened so I'd be led to this moment and this understanding.*

The next evening, when we had our nightly meeting, I stood and did a brief reading in front of the group. I began with, "My name is Mike, and I am an alcoholic." *Boom,* it felt as if an immense weight was lifted off my shoulders. Self-honesty produced a sense of freedom like nothing else had to that point.

Through the remainder of the program, I began talking and listening to Bill and John, a couple of gentlemen in the group who had experiences with the anonymous twelve-step program. Bill gave me an old copy of his book of program literature, writing a nice message for me inside the front cover. I began reading that book immediately.

Bill gave me some powerful advice. He said, "If or when someone asks you a question about something you don't know, just simply say, 'I don't know.'" This is very simple advice that makes a ton of sense.

John gave me good advice from what he had learned through his experiences in the program, and I was all ears. I can remember him saying, "You know Mike, the reason I share these things with you is because you listen. You don't say things like 'yeah but, yeah but.' You actually listen. That is pretty rare for a person your age." I appreciated that, and I truly was listening because I was eager to learn.

When I told John I'd begun to pray in the morning, asking God to help me to stay sober and to be an honest person just for today, John said, "That's great." Then he looked me right in the eye and said, "Do you have any leg or back problems?" When I said no, he said, "It doesn't hurt to get your knees dirty." Again, this was more simple advice that I followed. I realized that in my youth I had no excuse not to pray on my knees. I also realized that I was praying to something that I could not see, but had felt a presence, so I knew that something was hearing my prayers. John also mentioned how one of his advisers had told him to say a quick prayer prior to speaking. This was also great advice.

The last night of the two-week program was Friday, August 27. The counselors decided that it would be a good idea for us to chair our own meeting. I volunteered to speak, but I said that I wanted to speak last because I didn't want to take up too much time. Using the advice of my friend John, I said a quick prayer prior to speaking, and I asked God to help me share my experiences. This simple advice brought powerful results. I said a prayer, and then I stood and spoke. I did not need to over think things; I simply spoke of my experiences prior to the program, as well as what I had learned and experienced there.

One important thing I mentioned was how I intended to follow the simple twelve-step program as it is written. This program had worked for many others, and I didn't want to over think any of it, or act as if I were too smart for my own good. In short, I was not going to reinvent the wheel. One other important thing I touched upon was how I had always tried to be a good, honest person, but I realized I had been lying to myself for a long time, and it was time for me to start getting honest with myself. I could not expect to be able to be honest with other people if I didn't first learn to be honest with myself.

Another experience from this program that is worth mentioning is when one of the counselors brought up his wife. He said that when he asks her why she loves him she says, "Because you have a beautiful soul." This got me to thinking, *what about my soul!?* This insight also bore much fruit in the days, weeks, and months that followed.

The following morning was checkout day. I was excited to be going home, but also a little nervous because I knew my life was going to be different. I just did my best to stay positive, keep it simple and to enjoy the day rather than overwhelm myself by thinking too far ahead into the future. I decided I was going to live for the day and let tomorrow worry about itself. I am and will always be very grateful and humbled by my experience in that two-week program and all of the valuable life lessons I learned during that period of my life.

CHAPTER TWO

After the Program

SEPTEMBER

I exited the two-week program on Saturday, August 28, 2010. I was grateful to be able to see my girlfriend again and share my experiences from the previous two weeks. I told her about my *spiritual awakening*, and how I had decided I was going to follow a twelve-step program. I told her that it was going to be a different way of living, but somehow I felt that it would be better. I mentioned how I wanted to work the program so I could start sharing my message of hope and help other people with problems similar to my own. I was grateful for her understanding.

We went out for some breakfast; it was nice to eat a good meal. I downloaded an application on my cell phone that had prayers and meditations on it because I felt it would help me gain peace of mind. This application cost me $1.99, and it was one of the best investments I have ever made.

In the evening, I decided to heed the advice of one of the counselors from the program and go to a meeting in my area. Truth be told, it was not a very positive meeting. I did, however, meet a very positive influence, a man named Ed. One thing Ed would say was, "I made my peace with my Maker." He could recall the exact date and time the he made his peace. What I take from this is, *I have made my peace with my Maker; don't you think it would be wise for you to do the same!?* I am very grateful to Ed for the words of wisdom and guidance he provided me along my journey. I was unhappy after leaving that meeting, so I decided to take a break from meetings for a few days and continue reading the literature of the program and following the prayers. Since I had felt the touch of God's grace, I no longer enjoyed being around negative people. I visited my parents the following day (Sunday) for dinner, and I shared my experiences with them as well. I returned to work the following Monday, and I was happy to be back in the swing of things. I continued to read some literature each day so as to gain a better understanding of myself and the program as a whole. I followed the prayers and began to enjoy the simplicity of each day.

The following Friday, September 3, I decided to treat myself to some breakfast downtown prior to heading to work for the 3 p.m. to 11 p.m. shift. Afterwards, the thought came to me that I should treat myself to something nice. I remembered how as a child, my aunt had given me a chain with a pendant of Michael the Archangel. This pendant had brought me a great deal of blessings throughout my childhood, so I figured I would purchase a new one. I went into a jeweler in the downtown area and asked one of the staff members if they had a pendant of the Archangel. She said they had silver ones only, but since I had been saving a considerable amount of money in my new lifestyle, I said I wanted a gold one to match the chain I was wearing around my neck. (I had been wearing this chain for years; it held the number twelve and a cross.) She said, "Give me a minute," and went to check the store orders. She came back and said, "We actually ordered a few of those recently, and they should be in today." I was very happy to hear that and I thought, *Interesting; coincidence?* I left the store and returned about an hour later to make the purchase. I immediately added the pendant to my chain in between the cross and the number twelve.

Over the next couple of weeks, I continued my readings and following the prayers of the twelve-step program. In the beginning of my journey, I was staying at my girlfriend's apartment, so I would say my morning and evening prayers by the bedside. I continued to shop around and tried different meetings, and did my best to listen when others shared their life experiences, so I could continue to grow with an open mind. At this point, my understanding of the Creator was growing gradually. I realized that I could not see Him, but my life was somehow getting better.

I continued to grow gradually, one day at a time, and I started to notice things more clearly than I had before. Early on during the month of September, I started to notice the sixes (666) on license plates and on receipts wherever I would go. (666 is often associated with the devil). I thought to myself, *Wow, seeking a spiritual awakening is no joke!* There were also times during that month that I had bad dreams. These were not just dreams of drinking or using drugs, but dreams of battles of good versus evil. I can remember having a phone conversation with my mother where I said, "This stuff seems to make sense to me: twelve steps, the twelve apostles of Christ, the number twelve that I wore on my back through my careers of baseball and football, as well as the chain around my neck for a long time all seem to hold a lot of significance." She said, "Oh, you're just imagining things." I just responded with, "Okay."

In mid-September, I moved into a new apartment so I could be closer to my workplace. I settled into my new place, and I looked for meetings in the area. It just so happened that there was a meeting so close, that I could hit it with a snowball; another very interesting coincidence. I began attending this meeting roughly four or five times a week in order to learn more and be around honest, understanding people. I was especially interested in listening to the experienced members. It was at this meeting where I met one of the most positive people I have ever met—a man named Tom. I met Tom during my first meeting there, but I didn't get his phone number right away. I could tell from the first time I met him that he was clearly a person who had found the grace of God (or if you prefer, the Holy Spirit).

I enjoyed this group meeting in particular because there were many members of different ethnic backgrounds, genders, and accents who were willing to be honest with themselves and others. I also enjoyed the fact that most people were not denying God's grace. I can remember being in this meeting one morning and hearing a person say, "These steps should be done without delay." This helped me to open my mind some more, and I realized I needed to continue to grow. Within the next day or so, I purchased a copy of *Twelve Steps and Twelve Traditions*[1] and began reading it.

I can vividly remember going to a Friday night meeting with my friend Tom. The speaker was very positive, clearly a person who had found God's grace and serenity. Once the meeting was opened, I can recall some people speaking negatively about how upset they were and whatnot. I didn't feel negative or upset; I felt good. After the meeting, Tom took me aside and said, "The meetings are good, but the twelve steps and the program is what it's all about." This was very powerful, positive advice.

There were times during the month of September when I would pray at work in quiet places during the ungodly hours of the shift I was working. I can remember feeling the Spirit flow through me and around my body while praying. It felt like a warm breeze flowing through and through. It was very humbling, and I was grateful to be alive. I can remember saying, "God, now that I have found You, I can't let You go." At this point, my understanding of the Creator continued to grow, and I could see that the more effort and self-inquiry I was putting into the program, the more He would reward me openly. I could sense that I was growing closer to Him, because I began to feel His presence more often during prayer time and throughout the day.

One evening at work when I was on the 3 p.m. to 11 p.m. shift, I was sitting at a desk and I saw my cell phone light up at 9:07 p.m. This did not happen because of a message or missed call, so I thought, *Wow, that's interesting.* Immediately after that, I decided to open the application that I had on my phone for the King James Version of the Bible. I thought to open the application to Genesis 9:7 which reads, "And you, be ye fruitful, and multiply; bring forth abundantly in the earth, and multiply therein." *Wow,* I thought, *this seems like a little more than just a coincidence.* I decided that it was time to start sharing my experiences with my family and loved ones.

A few days after this occurrence, I had my mother over to my apartment for dinner. Prior to her arrival, I went to my quiet place of prayer (which is the bathroom in my apartment) and I prayed, "Father, please speak through me and help me share my experiences with my mom." When she came over, we had dinner, and then we sat down and had a talk. One of the things I can remember distinctly was her mention of my dad, and I said, "He is my earthly father; God is my heavenly Father." I didn't have to think about it; it just came out when I was speaking. (A month or so later, I read it in the Bible: "Do not call anyone on earth your father; for One is your Father, He who is in heaven" [Matthew 23:9]).

At any rate, our conversation went quite well, and she decided to accompany me to a meeting. Unfortunately, the meeting we went to was full of people who were still very much in the dark. Nonetheless, I had done the best I could. After the meeting, she and I were driving home and we stopped at a red light. I happened to look at the license plate of the car in front of us and the last three numbers were 777. (7 is the number of perfection, as God rested on the seventh day after creating everything in six. 777 is symbolic of the trinity; God the Father, the Son, and the Holy Spirit.) To some this may have seemed like a coincidence, but to me this was an indication that I was on the right path. Another thing I realized that evening with my mother was the fact that the more I spoke from experience, the more memories of significance began to come back to me.

Another day that sticks out vividly is Friday, September 24, 2010. On this day, I had my dad over to my apartment for a visit to share my experiences with him. Prior to his arrival, I went to my quiet place of prayer and I prayed, "Father, please help me to share my experiences with my dad. I know it's not going to be easy because we have a difficult time communicating with each other. Please allow me to drop his defenses with a handshake. Please God, I need You, if there is anything You can do to help. Jesus, I trust in You."

When my dad arrived, we decided to get breakfast at a small diner near my apartment. Once we were seated, my dad happened to notice a man sitting at the counter. This man's name was Peter. Peter and my dad had been good friends from decades past, and it turned out that they had almost lived together over thirty years ago. Certain life situations had prevented their living arrangements, but nonetheless, Peter came over to sit with us. It turns out that Peter had experienced some type of awakening years prior and realized that he was on somewhat of a destructive path, so he made a positive life change. Peter has been awake and sober-minded since the time of his realization, and I could tell based on how he spoke and the clarity of his eyes. After the three of us ate breakfast together, we had a very nice conversation. I can remember Peter said, "The psychosis of the twelve steps can be quite deep and very interesting if you follow them thoroughly." This was a wise and truthful statement. A little later, we parted ways and my dad and I returned to my apartment to have our own conversation. Again, I prayed quickly prior to our conversation and asked God to help me share my experiences with my dad. I shared with him as best I could, but I could tell based on the look in his eyes that he was not really following.

I recall saying, "Dad, do you think it's mere coincidence that Peter just happened to be there today?" Peter was the answer to the prayer I had said that morning. I also remember mentioning *The Four Agreements*[2] during our conversation and what a valuable book it is, containing simple life lessons. Once our conversation was over, I escorted him out of my apartment building to where his truck was parked. Just prior to him leaving, I shook his hand, and I could feel the Spirit exit my body through my hand and enter him. My dad nearly fell over backwards. The first words from his mouth after that handshake were, "Uh, huh, I'll read *The Four Agreements*!" As he was walking to his truck, he called me three or four different names before he called me "Mike." Clearly he felt the power of the Spirit, although, he later made no mention of it. Regardless of this, I know what I felt and what I experienced, and I know the Lord was with me on that day.

I continued growing spiritually, and going to meetings and reading literature, but it didn't seem to be enough. I decided it was time to get to work on my moral inventory. I tried to begin by writing out the seven deadly sins, but I kept hitting mental blocks. I tried calling advisers, and they just told me to write about anything that had been bothering me. I told one adviser that I had done a timeline during the two-week program, but something was telling me that I couldn't put a halfhearted effort into this. With nowhere else to turn, I took hold of the cross around my neck, and I prayed, "Father, please help me and guide me in the process of my moral inventory."

Upon saying this, I put the pen down and my brain instantly shifted back to the end of freshman year in high school, and memories just started coming back to me. I wrote for almost two weeks, spending a little time each day, until I felt as though I had been completely thorough and honest with myself. I then went back through it and added notes where necessary. Upon finishing this process, I went through the seven sins and was completely honest with myself as to how I had been guilty of committing each one. After completing this inventory, I felt much better mentally, physically, and spiritually. At this point in time, I began to realize that my Creator knew everything about me. This was a heavy thought at first, but I grew to appreciate this fact very much.

There were times during the month of September that I was completely overwhelmed by the presence of God (or if you prefer, the Holy Spirit). I can remember saying my nightly prayers in quiet places, and just crying because I was so grateful to have been saved through the grace of God. I can also remember hymns just coming to me, and at times I felt as though I was walking on air. I recall going to meetings in September and saying things like, "I'm really starting to appreciate God's greatest gift, my life." I can remember feeling so full of soul that I was going to float away. It was an awesome feeling, far greater than any drug or alcohol buzz.

Several more very important occurrences from the month of September are some e-mails that were sent back and forth between family, friends, and me:

September 27, 2010/9:23 a.m.

From me to Jon who is a friend of mine from college. The previous spring he visited the Wailing Wall in Israel, and he took with him a prayer I wrote for a man at my workplace who was suffering from a rare disease:

Hey Jon, it's been a while. I wanted to thank you again for passing on that prayer for me a few months ago. I would also like to say that it is a pleasure to see that you are fully enjoying God's greatest gift—your life. It saddens me to see so many squander this gift. I too was guilty of this in my past (it was basically a mere existence). Anyhow, I just wanted to say hello and it is great to see you are enjoying every day. Take care and God bless.—Mike

September 27/4:31 p.m.

From Jon:

Hey Mike, great to hear from you; you sound like a changed man. I hope you continue to seek God and grow in your faith. Take it day by day, that's all we can do. My life has been nothing but blessings since the day I saw the light and committed myself to living for God. I hope that our paths cross again in the not-too-distant future.—Blessings, Jon

This message got me to open my mind a little more. I thought, *Take it day by day* just like in a twelve-step program where we talk about living *One day at a time.* It also made me think, *What is my faith?* At this point in time it was just faith in God, but I'll explain my spiritual growth in the postscript of this book. I also wondered how the awakening happened for my friend, but I have yet to ask him details about it.

September 30/2:41 a.m.

From me:

Jon, that is so wonderful to hear! It's amazing when you finally wake up and realize that you have been living the life of your dreams, based on your own positive thoughts, or knowing that bad things happened based on negative thinking. The more unnecessary evils that I give up, the closer I feel to my Creator. I pray that we meet again, be it in this life or the next. Enjoy each moment, every smile, every embrace, and every kind act. God lives through good people who have faith. Take care and God bless.—Mike

Another event from September that really sticks out in my mind is an e-mail I received from my brother, Robert:

September 30/3:45 p.m.
From Robert:
Hey there! I picked up the *Salem News* this morning and this story really jumped out at me. Pretty amazing; there's got to be something to it. Take a look and let me know what you think!—Robert

My brother sent me a link to an online newspaper article. The gist of the article is that a builder found a two-thousand-year-old authentic silver shekel of Tyre while doing reconstruction work in Manchester, Massachusetts. Tyre was a Phoenician-Judean city which was located in present-day Lebanon. The shekel itself was minted between 126 BC and AD 66. The graven images on the shekel are of the Phoenician deity Melqart (Baal), on one side, and an Egyptian-style eagle with its right claw resting on a ship's rudder on the other side. The builder and the owner of the property where the shekel was found were trying to figure out how this coin could have ended up in Massachusetts. The property owner took the shekel to a coin and jewelry dealer, where it was inspected, weighed, and its authenticity was verified. It was noted that the coin had lost some of its mass over the years, but the Greek inscription "Tyre, the Holy and Inviolable" was still readable. The current property owner even rented a metal detector to search the property but found nothing else of significance. Below are some pieces of the article, followed by the response I sent my brother immediately after I had finished reading the article.

MANCHESTER—What a builder thought was a quarter has turned out to be a 2,000-year-old shekel, the kind of coin Judas was paid to betray Jesus . . . . [Phillip] Pelletier [the builder] said he is shocked he found a 2,000-year-old coin in Manchester but finds it ironic that he discovered the shekel on Holy Thursday, the day that commemorates the Last Supper of Jesus Christ with the Apostles; it was after the meal that Judas betrayed Christ . . . . "It's a complete mystery to me as to how it got there," Brewer-Siljeholm [the home owner] said . . . . "The only other plausible explanation I've heard to date is that a bird such as a seagull picked it up and dropped it there," Brewer-Siljeholm said. Pelletier also noted that it could have been buried or dug up from underground by a squirrel or other creature.[3]

September 30/3:58 p.m.

From me:

Wow, people can be so foolish, trying to find reason behind the unreasonable, questioning the unquestionable! A seagull or a squirrel—really!?! It seems that God is not happy with all of the sin in the world today. Murder, hate crimes, drugs, greed, lust, and selfishness. Please, follow the path to salvation; you have made great strides thus far. The Holy Spirit lives within me. I lost my way many times, but never lost faith in the Almighty. Please follow the steps and be made free.

In writing this response, I did not premeditate; I simply wrote it in the Spirit. As you, dear reader, can see, I was not very pleased upon reading this article. Honestly, how many signs must God give us? Some people simply have no faith, and I feel very sorry for those people. The answer to this "unsolved mystery" is that Christ is returning, and God the Father is trying to give us signs and clues to wake us up and lead us to salvation. These are the Scriptures regarding the silver shekel:

Then one of the twelve, called Judas Iscariot, went to the chief priests and said, "What are you willing to give me if I deliver Him to you?" And they counted out to him thirty pieces of silver. So from that time he sought opportunity to betray Him. (Matthew 26:14-16)

When morning came, all the chief priests and elders of the people plotted against Jesus to put Him to death. And when they had bound Him, they led Him away and delivered Him to Pontius Pilate the governor.

Then Judas, His betrayer, seeing that He had been condemned, was remorseful and brought back the thirty pieces of silver to the chief priests and elders, saying, "I have sinned by betraying innocent blood." And they said, "What is that to us? You see to it!" Then he threw down the pieces of silver in the temple and departed, and went and hanged himself.

But the chief priests took the silver pieces and said, "It is not lawful to put them into the treasury, because they are the price of blood." And they consulted together and bought with them the potter's field, to bury strangers in. Therefore that field has been called the Field of Blood to this day.

Then was fulfilled what was spoken by Jeremiah the prophet, saying, "And they took the thirty pieces of silver, the value of Him who was priced, whom they of the children of Israel priced, and gave them for the potter's field, as the LORD directed me." (Matthew 27:1-10)

Also, in regards to the image on the shekel, it is the image of a false god, Baal.

Now Ahaziah fell through the lattice of his upper room in Samaria, and was injured; so he sent messengers and said to them, "Go, inquire of Baal-Zebub, the god of Ekron, whether I shall recover from this injury." But the angel of the LORD said to Elijah the Tishbite, "Arise, go up to meet the messengers of the king of Samaria, and say to them, 'Is it because there is no God in Israel that you are going to inquire of Baal-Zebub, the god of Ekron?' Now therefore, thus says the LORD: 'You shall not come down from the bed to which you have gone up, but you shall surely die.'" So Elijah departed.

And when the messengers returned to him, he said to them, "Why have you come back?" So they said to him, "A man came up to meet us, and said to us, 'Go, return to the king who sent you, and say to him, "Thus says the LORD: 'Is it because there is no God in Israel that you are sending to inquire of Baal-Zebub, the god of Ekron? Therefore you shall not come down from the bed to which you have gone up, but you shall surely die.'"'"

Then he said to them, "What kind of man was it who came up to meet you and told you these words?" So they answered him, "A hairy man wearing a leather belt around his waist." And he said, "It is Elijah the Tishbite." Then the king sent to him a captain of fifty with his fifty men. So he went up to him; and there he was, sitting on the top of a hill. And he spoke to him: "Man of God, the king has said, 'Come down!'"

So Elijah answered and said to the captain of fifty, "If I am a man of God, then let fire come down from heaven and consume you and your fifty men." And fire came down from heaven and consumed him and his fifty. Then he sent to him another captain of fifty with his fifty men. And he answered and said to him: "Man of God, thus has the king said, 'Come down quickly!'" So Elijah answered and said to them, "If I am a man of God, let fire come down from heaven and consume you and your fifty men." And the fire of God came down from heaven and consumed him and his fifty. Again, he sent a third captain of fifty with his fifty men. And the third captain of fifty went up, and came and fell on his knees before Elijah, and pleaded with him, and said to him: "Man of God, please let my life and the life of these fifty servants of yours be precious in your sight. Look, fire has come down from heaven and burned up the first two captains of fifties with their fifties. But let my life now be precious in your sight."

And the angel of the LORD said to Elijah, "Go down with him; do not be afraid of him." So he arose and went down with him to the king. Then he said to him, "Thus says the LORD: 'Because you have sent messengers to inquire of Baal-Zebub, the god of Ekron, is it because there is no God in Israel to inquire of His word? Therefore you shall not come down from the bed to which you have gone up, but you shall surely die.'"

So Ahaziah died according to the word of the LORD which Elijah had spoken. (2 Kings 1:2-17)

There is the answer to this "unsolved mystery"; a sign from our Creator, or if you prefer, a wake-up call of Christ's return. Baal-Zebub was a false god (Baal-Zebub = Beelzebub). If you are further interested in the false god Baal-Zebub, see 1 Kings 18:20-40. In closing about this article, I know it's not always easy to believe in something that you cannot see, which is why God gives us signs to warn us. It just makes me sad to see how spiritually blind and faithless some people are.

Another experience that I can remember from September 2010 was when I had finished my thorough moral inventory and decided to do my fifth step (which was to read my moral inventory out loud). I did this on a Saturday; I believe it was September 25. I went to one of the Catholic churches in the area and sat down with a priest. I did this because as a child I was brought up around the Catholic Church. I sat down with the priest and read my entire confession out loud. The look in his eyes was unforgettable. I doubt he had heard such a thorough confession before.

But you, O man of God, flee these things and pursue righteousness, godliness, faith, love, patience, gentleness. Fight the good fight of faith, lay hold on eternal life, to which you were also called and have confessed the good confession in the presence of many witnesses. (1 Timothy 6:11-12)

Once I had finished speaking he asked, "So how is it now?" I responded, "How is what?" He said, "The sex." I was quite appalled that my sex life was all he had gathered from my confession, so I asked him, "This is the day the Lord has made; to what day is this in reference?" He said, "The day we are in." I said, "Absolutely. For a long time I was under the false assumption that it was referring to Christmas Day or Easter Sunday." I then said to him, "Through Him, with Him, and in Him; who are they talking about?" and he said, "Jesus." I said, "I am fairly certain that this is in reference to human beings, not just Jesus. Jesus was God, living as a man!" He disagreed, and I said, "Well then how come when I pray I feel the presence of the Spirit? How can you explain how I was able to write such a thorough confession?"

He didn't have much of a response, and shortly after, the priest "absolved me" of my sins. I had almost considered going for confirmation, but I realized I did not need a man to try to give me something (the Holy Spirit) that I had already received from God. After I left my confession, I thought about the difference between faith and religion. I thought to myself that I no longer want to be involved in any particular religion. I am no longer about religion; I am a man of faith and spirituality, just as a twelve-step program is about faith and spirituality, not religion. I understood that I was developing a relationship with God, not a religion.

OCTOBER

Friday October 1 is a date that I will not soon forget. After some careful planning during the month of September and shopping around, I had found the perfect engagement ring for my girlfriend. I picked it up on the morning of the first, using the utmost discretion, and I was quite nervous. One of her best friends helped me pick out the perfect ring. Once I got back home to my apartment, I went to my quiet place and prayed.

During this prayer session, I was giving thanks to God. I was actually crying at the time because I could feel the overwhelming presence of the Spirit, and I was so thankful for all of the positive changes that were happening in my life. Without premeditating anything, the words, "Father please take this body and do with me as Thou wilt," just came out of my mouth. Looking back, I had read it weeks prior, and I will share it with you here:

We were now at Step Three: Many of us said to our Maker, as we understood Him: "God, I offer myself to Thee—to build with me and do with me as Thou wilt. Relieve me of the bondage of self, that I may better do Thy will. Take away my difficulties, that victory over them may bear witness to those I would help of Thy Power, Thy Love, and Thy Way of life. May I do Thy will always!" We thought well before taking this step making sure we were ready; that we could at last abandon ourselves utterly to Him.

We found it very desirable to take this spiritual step with an understanding person, such as our wife, best friend, or spiritual adviser. But it is better to meet God alone than with someone who might misunderstand. The wording was, of course, quite optional so long as we expressed the idea, voicing it without reservation. This was only a beginning, though if honestly and humbly made, an effect, sometimes a very great one, was felt at once.[4]

Upon saying this, I felt Spirit enter me through the top of my head. I could feel (painless) shifting going on in my brain. I recall saying to my girlfriend, "Uh oh, something just happened!" She didn't quite understand, and really, neither did I at the time. (Looking back, it was one of the best things I have ever done for myself, and the truth is, the shifting I felt was God restoring me to sanity and filling in the holes I had put in my brain through the abuse of mind-altering chemicals.)

Later on that afternoon, my lady and I went out to dinner at the restaurant where we had our first date. I had the ring in my pocket, and I excused myself to the men's room to wash my face and calm myself. I was somewhat nervous because I wanted to make it a memorable proposal. Rather than panic, I simply asked the Spirit to speak through me. Returning to the table, I got down on one knee and proposed to my lady. I can still remember the words that came out of my mouth, as well as her response to the ring and the proposal, but I'm going to keep that little piece to myself.

After dinner, my newly engaged fiancée and I thought it would be fun to go see a psychic. Although I would not recommend this to everyone because I am not an advocate of the occult, I am going to include this particular occurrence. The woman I sat down with was very positive and very spiritual. She gave me a great deal of insight to the questions I asked her, and she could absolutely tell I had been having some major spiritual experiences. While seated, she had me put my hands over her crystal. Once I removed my hands, she looked into her crystal. After a brief moment, she looked right up at me with her eyes wide open. She said, "Wow! You've just come from a very dark place, haven't you?!" I said, "Yes, I have." She said, "You've been found, haven't you?" I said, while pointing upward, "Yes, He saved me." I could tell by the look in her eyes that she knew that I had found God.

I recall her saying, "There are two spirits protecting you. One of them is a female, and she's been watching over you since birth." I asked, "Is it the Holy Mother?" And she said, "If that is your faith, then yes." She told me there was also a spirit of a young man who had been watching over me. I understood this to be my friend Christopher. Chris was a good friend from college, and he was one of my linemen on the football team; he also tutored me in calculus and other subjects. Chris died during an unusual accident aboard the shipping vessel he was working on. I have kept his picture and his obituary card; I still have it to this day. He was a real sweetheart of a young man. At any rate, as I continued with the psychic, she pulled her Tarot cards. Saint Michael the Archangel came up between five and seven times. She then said, "The Archangel Michael has also been closely watching over you." I then said, "I wear his pendant around my neck and I often ask him to intervene on the Lord's behalf." I told her how on occasion I would ask the archangel to strike negative thoughts from my head. She looked at me with her eyes wide open and said, "Wow!"

Shortly after, she said something like, "Feel the positive light energy." I interrupted her and said, "You are talking about God, the Father. He is an invisible God. He is a Spirit." She just looked at me with her eyes wide open and said, "Okay." She could tell that I knew a few things, some of which, I didn't even realize at that time. Next, I asked her a few questions that had been on my mind. I asked, "Can you tell me about the silver shekel that was found in Manchester?" I had read the article and was interested. She said, "You were supposed to see that. I am guessing that you were somewhat upset when you saw that article." I said, "Yes, I was; it seemed like quite an obvious sign."

I then asked her about the Apocalypse and the end times. She said, "It might not happen exactly as most people think. People who have lived for wealth and socioeconomic status, um, they are going to be very sorry. Correct me if I'm wrong, but you've been somewhat of a warrior all of your life, have you not? You have been in many leadership roles, perhaps both athletically and academically. You may have even been in the military?" I said, "Wow, now that you mention it, I have; and yes I did go to a military school, although I never served actively." She said, "Interesting." I then told her about the spiritual journey of faith I had been on. I told her how I had been embracing a lot of change in a short period of time, and it was not always easy. She then asked, "What month were you born in?" I said, "February." She said, "That makes you a Pisces, and as a Pisces you have a tendency to try to please everyone and allow others to affect your decision making. That could make this journey somewhat difficult for you."

I then told her how good God had been to me, and I said, "God has been taking care of me so I will just remain faithful to Him, but I need to continue growing and embracing positive changes." She said, "Think of Psalm 23: The Lord is my shepherd, I shall not want."

(Psalm 23 has given me so much peace of mind along my journey.) She then told me that I would most likely start having visions, either through meditation or through dreams. I thought, *Wow, that's good news.* The session ended shortly after this. She wished me well and told me, "God bless." I thanked her for her insight and said, "May God bless you as well."

The following day, October 2, was a great day. I began to really feel the healing powers of the Spirit. I felt very positive, and I was gaining a better understanding of life. I began to understand that the Creator was healing me from the inside out. Some of the ideas I spoke of are written in a book called *The Secret*[5] by Rhonda Byrne. I began to understand the secret prior to reading the book. I began to feel less hungry because it seemed as though I was being nourished from the inside out. I recall going to dinner that evening with my family to celebrate my dad's birthday. I remember feeling somewhat judgmental, witnessing all of the gluttony that was going on around me, but I realized that I had no right to judge anyone except myself; however, I must say that sin began to stand out to me like never before. All in all, it was pleasant to be around my family, but it was very difficult to share my spiritual experiences with them.

Following dinner, my family headed to my sister's house for birthday cards and presents, etc. I can recall having a very nice conversation with my aunt, who had some experience with the twelve-step program I was currently in. We shared some experiences, as well as some of the miracles we had witnessed in regards to answered prayers and other positive happenings under the grace of God. She told me about an instance where she had been praying about her mother (my grandmother), and after she prayed, she found an old patch with her name on it which she had not seen in years. I remember her mention how she had been having some trouble with finances as of late. I simply told her, "Well, Aunty, don't underestimate the power of a positive prayer." She decided to take my advice, and as we move forward, I will share what transpired.

The following day, Sunday, my aunt and my sister decided to come by my apartment for coffee so we could continue our conversation from the night before. We each shared some insight in regards to our life experiences, and I shared with them some of the spiritual experiences I had been having. It was a very positive get together, and I was grateful to have had the opportunity to share my experience, strength, and hope with my loved ones. After they left, I can remember sitting on my couch and meditating for nearly an hour. (It really seemed like I had slept with my eyes open, and when I came to, the room was full of light.) I still cannot offer any explanation for this.

I headed to work that evening for the overnight shift (11 p.m.-7 a.m.). I can remember feeling a nice spiritual buzz while at work, and one of my coworkers asked me what I was smiling about. I said, "You wouldn't believe me if I told you." I decided to send my sister (Stephanie) a message from work during break time. These are e-mails back and forth between my sister and me:

October 4/3:13 a.m.
From me:

Hey Steph, I just wanted to say that it was an absolute pleasure hanging out and talking with you and Aunty on Sunday. I hope that we have many more occasions like that in the future. I love you very much, and I hope you have a great day and week. ☺—Mike

October 5/9:36 a.m.
From Stephanie:

Hey brother, I have to agree; I left your apartment feeling a sense of enlightenment that I haven't felt in a very long time. I almost feel like you and I now have a new and improved relationship, one that I look forward to sharing for a lifetime. You are a blessing to me and I love you very much.

I received another message from my sister the following day.

October 6/8:04 p.m.

From Stephanie:

Aunty has some great news. She said that you and she talked about something work related on Sunday and she can't wait to tell you what transpired these past few days after praying about it. I'm going to e-mail her your cell phone number, so expect to hear from her so she can share her good news. Love you!

Now, what happened is quite simple, dear reader, and I shall share it with you now. My aunt prayed for something she needed to help her and her family—not a selfish want, but a need. The following day at work, her boss mentioned giving her some more hours on the books. Interesting, don't you think? A day or two after this, while at work, she received a phone call from the principal of one of the high schools in her area. The principal asked my aunt if her company would be interested in taking on a project for this particular school. My aunt mentioned it to her boss, and her boss was astonished. Her boss couldn't believe it, since the company had been trying to get a contract with that particular school for over a decade. Her boss then asked her if she would mind working full-time. Some would say this is a mere coincidence, but as I understand it, this was the handiwork of the Good Shepherd.

I continued to grow in my faith through the month of October. By this point in time, I had read nearly every piece of literature the twelve-step program had to offer, which increased my spiritual growth and led me into the Holy Bible. It's funny, prior to having a spiritual awakening I thought the Bible was a religious book merely written by mortal men. As I got into it, however, I realized that it is a book of spiritual faith with many simple, valuable life lessons. The men and women who wrote the Bible had had different types of spiritual experiences which were recorded into a book. "All Scripture is given by inspiration of God, and is profitable for doctrine, for reproof, for correction, for instruction in righteousness, that the man of God may be complete, thoroughly equipped for every good work" (2 Timothy 3:16-17). I am grateful to have found out through experience that the Bible has little or nothing to do with religion.

I started reading the Bible the easiest way I knew how, which is how I would recommend anyone begin; with the Gospels. I prefer the copies which contain the words of Jesus in red. I remember reading the book of John and writing out some of the words spoken by Jesus. I began studying the parables, and they seemed to make a lot of sense to me as I continued to wake up spiritually. (A parable is an earthly story with a spiritual truth.) I found the four Gospels to be the easiest place to start, and my reason is simple. Accounts of Jesus's life are found in different Gospels, each written from the perspective of the Gospel's author. The different versions are quite similar, but not identical. It is as if you, dear reader, and I were to witness an event (say a movie, a play, or an athletic event) and then each write a recap of what we had seen. Our accounts of the event would not be exactly the same even though we had witnessed the same event.

It saddens my soul to hear a person say, "I don't believe in Jesus" when that person hasn't even read the Gospels. I can understand though, because prior to waking up and actually looking into His teachings for myself, I wasn't sure what to believe. However, rather than being ignorant about the subject, I decided to take a firsthand look. It seems that many people witnessed His life, and then they wrote about it after the fact. I am grateful to have been open-minded enough to read these for myself rather than rely on someone else's opinion. This type of situation reminds me of the story about a man who said he didn't like to read; this man had at least read a book prior to making that decision.

During the second week of October, I remembered a book I had purchased two months prior by a Christian pastor. The title of this book was *What in the World Is Going On?* written by Dr. David Jeremiah. In this book, Dr. Jeremiah dissects and breaks down the book of Daniel—one of the Lord's finest prophets—and how historical events that have already taken place match up with what is written in that book. Reading the pastor's book enabled me to gain a much clearer understanding of the book of Daniel. The pastor's book was so intriguing and well written that I couldn't put it down. I read it cover to cover in slightly over a day. This is one particular quote that the pastor makes reference to which I can completely relate to based on my life experiences:

The average age of the world's greatest civilizations from the beginning of history has been about 200 years. During those 200 years, these nations always progressed through the following sequence:

> From bondage to spiritual faith;
> From spiritual faith to great courage;
> From courage to liberty;
> From liberty to abundance;
> From abundance to complacency;
> From complacency to apathy;
> From apathy to dependence;
> From dependence back into bondage.[7]

Based on my own life experiences in this world and in this country (USA) I would say that we are currently in a state of dependence. In my experience, my generation is entirely dependent on Oil, technology, alcohol, socioeconomic status, worshipping money, pornography, television shows with graphic immorality (shows that promote alcoholism, atheism, and racism; shows where young people actually get paid to spread the filth to America's youth), and overall negativity. I'll admit, I used to think some of these programs were funny as well, until I decided to get my mind out of the gutter and realized just how insulting these shows are to a healthy, happy, positive way of life, and how the messages brought forth in certain programs was searing my conscience and filling my head with mindless filth. But hey, what would I know; I've only lived through it all. It makes me think of the following Scripture: "For what will it profit a man if he gains the whole world, and loses his own soul? Or what will a man give in exchange for his soul? For whoever is ashamed of Me and My words in this adulterous and sinful generation, of him the Son of Man also will be ashamed when He comes in the glory of His Father with the holy angels"(Mark 8:36-38).

Dr. Jeremiah also brings up the question of whether or not America has a role in the prophecy. In my reading, I was quite certain that we do, but at that point in time I wasn't quite sure yet. The ending chapter of the pastor's book is entitled "The Return of the King" in which he writes of Christ's glorious return to earth. For now, that is all that I shall mention about the pastor's book and my experiences while reading it.

After reading Dr. Jeremiah's book, I went ahead and read the book of Daniel in the Old Testament. I actually read through it a couple of times. It makes a great deal of sense to me now, even some of the dates and numbers which the pastor had not mentioned in his book. However, my goal is not to start trying to pinpoint dates; it's just to share the truth with you.

Throughout October, I continued to grow along spiritual lines and develop a closer relationship with my Creator. In the beginning of my journey, I just called Him God and Father. There came a point early in October, when I decided to print out a list of the names of God and mix it up a little with my prayers. A simple example of a morning prayer for me during this period of my journey was as follows: "Good morning, Alpha, this is Michael. Please help me to stay sober and be a truthful, honest person, just for today. For it is Your will, not mine, be done, Amen." I continued to use His different names during my prayer time to see His response and which ones He prefers most. In my experience, God goes by many different names, but there is only one God.

As I continued to grow on my journey of faith, I began to see everything more clearly. I was really living in life, rather than merely existing. I could view situations and understand why things are as they are. It seemed as though I had a new set of eyes to see with. Life was getting better by the day, and I really began to appreciate every moment of it.

Through the advice and good counsel of my fiancée, I decided it best to continue to seek knowledge through spiritual authors. I enjoy reading these books because I find spiritual authors to be very truthful people who understand life. Although I had begun to get very deep into the Bible at this point, I figured it wouldn't hurt to be spiritually rounded. One book that caught my eye was *Future Tense*[8] by Rabbi Jonathan Sacks. Rabbi Sacks is a very wise man, and I thoroughly enjoyed reading his book. It seems to me that through prayer, some research, an open mind, and my readings of authors of different faiths, that there is only one God. The Rabbi makes many references to the Hebrew Torah, which is the first five books of the Old Testament, written by Moses. The Rabbi mentions the Divine Presence, which in my understanding, is the same as the Holy Spirit (in Christian terminology), or what the member of a twelve-step program would refer to as The Miracle. Simply put, it is the presence of God, or if you prefer, the grace of God. I learned quite a bit from Rabbi Sacks, and I am grateful for his teachings.

In the mid to latter half of October, I continued to attend meetings of the twelve-step program. One in particular stands out in my memory. While I was listening to other members, I said a quick prayer in my head prior to it being my turn to speak and asked the Spirit to speak through me. Once it was my turn to speak I stood up and said, "My name is Michael. I am a creation of the Lord. What I have found is what a Jew would refer to as the Divine Presence, a Christian would call the Holy Spirit, or what we of the twelve-steps would refer to as The Miracle. Correct me if I'm wrong, but when cut do we not all bleed the same color red? If we were to cry, would the tears not be of the same saline solution? I cannot expect someone else to know exactly as I know or think exactly as I think; it is part of the dignity of difference. I have taken the principles of this program completely to heart: *Don't Drink*—I made the decision to stop drinking. *Go to Meetings*—I started going to meetings. *Ask for Help*—I ask God for help every morning, and I thank Him every night. When I worked my fourth step, I sincerely prayed and asked God to help me with my moral inventory, and the memories just started coming back to me."

Some people listened, but some people did not. Quite a shame, considering the wise ones had already been saved through faith and the Spirit. It somewhat brought my spirit down to see how many "deaf" people there were in that very room. I thought everyone understood, but I realized that I had probably been a little more thorough in my self-evaluation than most others, it is possible that my faith was deeper than that of most people. While sitting in meetings, I did a great deal of listening so I could continue to grow and attain wise counsel.

More memories came back to me as I continued to grow spiritually in my faith through the month of October. One thing I came to realize, the more I grew in faith, is how good my life has been. I shared some of this with my parents and my fiancée during the latter half of October. It was after a dinner between the four of us that I shared my life story. Prior to sharing, I went out on the back porch of my parents' house, knelt down, and asked the Spirit to speak through me to help me share my experiences. I spoke to them for almost forty-five minutes and shared my life story, beginning with my childhood. Once I had finished, it was very clear to me that I had been living my own dream. Some parts of my dream have been better than others, depending on positive or negative decisions I had made. This was a vast, eye-opening realization for me.

Another memory that stands out vividly from my journey occurred on Wednesday, October 27. On this particular day, my fiancée and I went to visit one of my college professors and his wife. I had been looking forward to this rendezvous because this particular professor had been a very positive influence in my life. Also, he has been in the twelve-step program for nearly twenty-five years, so I figured he might understand the spiritual experiences I was having. This day did not go quite as well as I thought it would. During this visit, I treated him and his wife with nothing but respect, kindness, and compassion. I shared my entire experience over lunch, and his wife proceeded to pass judgment on both my fiancée and me. She continued to call my fiancée by the wrong name, and she was quite ignorant towards the nice young couple she had invited into her home. It's a shame when negative people pass judgment on people who speak truthfully and show kindness.

I tried to explain that in thoroughly working the twelve steps I have been reborn, and I have a clear conscience again—the voice of reason,

God's voice in my head. From the apostle Paul: "I thank God, whom I serve with a pure conscience, as my forefathers did, as without ceasing I remember you in my prayers night and day" (2 Timothy 1:3). She obviously did not have the ears to hear. I wasn't overly happy about this particular experience, but I decided to take the advice of Jesus: "And when you go into a household, greet it. If the household is worthy, let your peace come upon it. But if it is not worthy, let your peace return to you. And whoever will not receive you nor hear your words, when you depart from that house or city, shake off the dust from your feet" (Matthew 10:12-14).

I felt somewhat disheartened from this visit, because I had wanted to catch up with my old professor (whom I haven't spoken to since). I was astounded because in weeks prior, his wife had given me the advice, via telephone, to remain open-minded, and I witnessed firsthand her being very closed-minded. Perhaps she didn't believe my story because I am much younger than she is. This, also, makes me think of the apostle Paul's advice: "Let no one despise your youth, but be an example to the believers in word, in conduct, in love, in spirit, in faith, in purity" (1 Timothy 4:12). It is a shame how pride, ego, and negativity can become part of a person's normal thought process as we age. I know this from experience because I used to be prideful and ignorant as well, but the grace of God has helped me to unlearn that very quickly.

The following day is one I will not soon forget. In adhering to the teachings of Jesus, I was able to maintain a positive frame of mind. I was on a spiritual high. In remaining positive and faithful, I was able to help many people. I started the day off with my morning prayer and a morning meeting. Then I decided to knock on the door of one of my neighbors (Jake). Jake invited me into his apartment, and he shared some gospel music with me. I remember being very moved while listening to this music because I was so grateful to have been saved through God's grace. Next, we went to a social commitment, and I shared my positive message of hope through the grace of God and the Holy Spirit, and it seemed to help some of the people who were there to listen.

From there, we decided to get some lunch. I recall looking at him and saying, "Jake, I'm not hungry, but if you want to eat, that's fine." The truth is, I was not hungry at all because I felt completely full of soul: "For the bread of God is He who comes down from heaven and gives life to the world." Then they said to Him, "Lord, give us this bread always." And Jesus said to them, "I am the bread of life. He who comes to Me shall never hunger, and he who believes in Me shall never thirst" (John 6:33-35). In my understanding, I was being filled with the Bread of Life because I was helping people and sharing positive energy with others. I also remembered how one of the instructors from the two-week program had said, "Think of Mother Teresa." I thought, *Wow, she must have felt like this every day. What an awesome way to live.*

After Jake and I had lunch, we went to visit his ex-wife, Carla, who had been down on her luck. I remember being on a wonderful spiritual high this day, and it felt as if I were walking on air. When we got to Carla's apartment building, we walked in through a courtyard. As we were about to enter through the vestibule, the doors opened for us. These were not automatic doors, so I was quite amazed by this. We went to the elevator and headed up to Carla's apartment. As we entered her apartment, I could literally feel her sadness. I could tell she was a woman of faith because there were Bibles and Scripture everywhere. The three of us held hands, and Jake said a prayer. This prayer seemed to offer only a little help to Carla. I could feel the sadness of this woman, whom I had not met prior to this encounter, in the pit of my stomach. I could sense that she needed to cry, and in truth, I could feel it.

She and Jake continued to talk, when the thought popped into my head, *What would Jesus do?* I immediately humbled myself to my knees and prayed for her out loud, "Abba, Father, please bless this woman and help her to see herself as You and I see her, a beautiful woman of Your creation who just needs a break, and a little positive guidance." After I finished praying, she began to cry, and I cried with her. It felt wonderful to help relieve her of her negative, bottled-up emotions. She gave me a hug, and I continued to cry with her for a moment. She thanked me and I responded by saying, "It was the very least I could do." Jake and I left shortly after and continued on our day of helping others (working for God). Jake later told me that Carla had not cried in years, and she has not been the same woman since that day. I knew it was the power of the Holy Spirit working through me—I did not have to think, I knew, based on what the Spirit told me through my soul, my emotions, and my conscience.

As we continued in our travels that day, Jake and I went to a hospital to give his friend (and spiritual adviser) a haircut. I could see that the hospital was not taking adequate care of this man. While we sat in the room, I could hear the man in the bed next to Jake's friend cry out. I went over to him and asked if he needed help. He said, "Yes!" and I immediately went out into the corridor to get assistance for him. I said to one of the two nurses standing outside the room, "Excuse me, this man needs help." The nurse replied, "Yeah, okay," and then continued to gossip with the other nurse. I interrupted, "Excuse me! There is a human being in here that needs your help! Isn't that why you're here? To help people!?" I could tell she did not like what I had to say; some people do not like to hear the truth.

After she checked on him, I went over to this man's bed, knelt beside him, and prayed; that is all I could do. Once Jake had finished cutting his friend's hair, he cleaned up and we were about to leave the hospital. I then said, "Jake, I'd like to say a prayer before we leave." He said, "Okay, you lead." We knelt beside his friend's bed, and I prayed from my heart without premeditation, "Abba, Father, please bless this man and grant him comfort and peace in his day as we await the glorious cry of the Archangel, when the trumpet sounds, and You call us up; and we will walk, hand in hand, in the days when the last shall be first, and the first shall be last." This prayer just came out, partially because I too am eager for the day when there shall be no more sin, no more greed, and the people who have chosen to live selfishly and walk all over others will be dealt with accordingly. It made me upset to see nurses who seemed to have forgotten the reason why they had become nurses: to help people and provide care for patients. After we finished the prayer for Jake's friend, Jake and I left the hospital, and I returned home for the evening. Once I got home I thought, *Wow, I wish every day presented so many opportunities to help other people.*

Friday, October 29, was a day that I was scheduled to work the 3 p.m. to 11 p.m. shift. In the morning before heading to work, I decided to watch *The Passion of the Christ.*[9] I had seen this movie before, but this was the first time I watched it since I had awoken spiritually. I noticed much more in the movie this time because it seemed like I was seeing it with different eyes. One scene in the movie (although the entire movie is very moving and powerful) caught my eyes and ears in particular. Jesus is seated amongst His apostles and He says, "You must not be afraid. The Helper will come who reveals the truth about God and who comes from the Father." I thought, *Wow! Maybe I am supposed to be seeing this.* I paused the movie and went to my quiet place of prayer to call on the Lord, except this time, I used the names for Him that Jesus used, and I pronounced them the same way He does in the movie. I prayed, "Adonai, I thank You, Father, for showing this to me." As soon as I said the name "Adonai," He hit me with so much Spirit that I was nearly knocked from my knees. I thought, *Wow, apparently He really likes that name.* Since that experience, whenever I pray I call on Him via His original names.

As October came to a close, I continued to grow in my faith. One thing that became very clear to me was that God had been doing positive things for me and helping me make positive life changes which I could not possibly have done on my own. No amount of willpower was going to help me enjoy my life more; it required God's-power. "With men this is impossible, but with God all things are possible" (Matthew 19:26).

NOVEMBER

During the month of November, the Holy Spirit continued to grow inside me. I would speak the Word of God (simply telling the truth based on my life experiences), but unfortunately I found this was not bringing the results I had hoped for. I would share the good news and all of the knowledge and wisdom I had gained from the Spirit, and people just looked at me cross-eyed. I continued to try to share the truth at twelve-step meetings, as well as with my family. I tried to share the Word with people at work, but they did not want to listen. My friends and family continued to doubt and even ignore me. I found this quite baffling; however, I found my answer in the following Scriptures:

> So they were offended at Him. But Jesus said to them, "A prophet is not without honor except in his own country and in his own house." (Matthew 13:57)

> But Jesus said to them, "A prophet is not without honor except in his own country, among his own relatives, and in his own house." (Mark 6:4)

> Therefore I speak to them in parables, because seeing they do not see, and hearing they do not hear, nor do they understand. And in them the prophesy of Isaiah is fulfilled, which says: *"Hearing you will hear and shall not understand, and seeing you will see and not perceive; for the hearts of this people have grown dull. Their ears are hard of hearing, and their eyes they have closed, lest they should see with their eyes and hear with their ears, lest they should understand with their hearts and turn, so that I should heal them."* (Matthew 13:13-15)

> For there is nothing hidden which will not be revealed, nor has anything been kept secret but that it should come to light. If anyone has ears to hear, let him hear." (Mark 4:22-23)

Being truthful and sharing my faith brought me some trouble in my place of work as well. On one occasion I was sharing some knowledge with my supervisor, a man whom I had been honest with in the days prior to finding the Holy Spirit. As I was speaking to him, the sun shone through the cracks of the shades in his office and directly on my face. Naturally, he did not notice this. It did seem, however, that he was very intrigued with what I shared with him. I shared as much as I could because during this time, I felt completely saturated with the Spirit and full of joy, love, and compassion. I was compelled to share the Word of God. He then asked me if I would mind sharing my experience with some other people at work, namely, the doctors. Being very naive, I thought that these educated men would actually listen when I spoke.

Prior to meeting these doctors, I did what I always do in such circumstances. I said a quick prayer, "Abba, please speak through me and help me to share my experiences with these gentlemen." I relate this to the teachings of Paul: "Let no corrupt word proceed out of your mouth, but what is good for necessary edification, that it may impart grace to the hearers"(Ephesians 4:29). Once we were all seated, I began by showing them a piece of my moral inventory (or if you prefer, my confession) from my fourth and fifth steps, to show them that I was telling the truth. This was a huge mistake on my part. These doctors were not looking to listen to me at all. They were looking to diagnose a young man who needed no diagnosis. This reminds me of the following Scriptures: "Those who are well have no need of a physician, but those who are sick" (Matthew 9:12). In this Scripture, Jesus is referring to people being spiritually sick (doubtful, negative, foolish, and sinful); spiritually deaf and blind; and not being able to hear and understand when a person is speaking the truth. Honestly, I was trying to help the doctors, but they were not willing or able to listen. They persecuted me for my honesty and my faith.

This situation also reminded me of The Proverbs of King Solomon: "A wise man will hear and increase learning, and a man of understanding will attain wise counsel, to understand a proverb and an enigma, the words of the wise and their riddles. The fear of the LORD is the beginning of knowledge, but fools despise wisdom and instruction" (Proverbs 1:5-7). I also pointed out the article from the *Salem News*, regarding the silver shekel, to these doctors so they could read it for themselves. My supervisor appeared somewhat disappointed, because it seemed as though he was interested in what I was saying, and he thought the doctors would actually listen and be interested as well. At any rate, this encounter obviously did not go as well as I had hoped, but I decided to keep a positive frame of mind.

Shortly after this encounter, for some strange reason, I decided to volunteer for an MRI. The doctors seemed very concerned in my mentioning the shifting I had felt in my head. They plainly did not want to listen when I told them it was the Holy Spirit restoring me to sanity. I figured my best bet would be to provide some visual proof.

On Saturday the thirteenth, I went in for an MRI. I had volunteered for this, mostly because I wanted to see what my brain looked like. I received the image results only a few days later. What I saw was enough proof for me: a full, symmetrical brain covered with the white light of the Holy Spirit. My nasal passages which had been healed and restored through the healing powers of the Spirit, and the eye sockets which looked like two headlights of bright white light. I was eager to hear the medical explanations for this.

I was ordered by the work doctors to go and see my primary care physician (PCP). Adhering to their advice, I made an appointment and went to see my PCP. When the doctor entered the examination room, he said, "You're fine; there's nothing wrong with you." I said, "Okay, can you tell me what you saw in the images?" He responded, "I didn't even look at the images." I was not amused by this to say the least. I had invested time and money to get the MRI, missed some hours at work, paid more money to see my PCP, and yet received zero information. I tried to share my experiences with my PCP (a man whom I thought I could trust, since I had known him for years), and just like the work doctors, he treated me as if there were something wrong with me because I spoke of spiritual things. I was quite disappointed by this, but I figured that would be the end of the doctor endeavors.

In the upcoming weeks, I was told to go see the doctors at work again. Prior to one visit, I had my hearing checked at the medical center at work. I work in a very loud environment with vibrating equipment, so after a year on the job, my hearing had become slightly impaired. I was now two years into this job, so I was interested to see the results of this hearing test. Just as I suspected, my hearing was as good, if not better, than it was prior to me beginning this job two years before. I knew that this was due to the healing powers of the Holy Spirit. As expected, the two doctors had no explanation for it. They offered a lot of "We think" and "It could be because of . . ." and other nonsense of the like. I explained to them that I still listened to loud music, except now it was good music. (I'll provide a list of some of these songs in chapter 5.) These genius doctors still had not looked at the pictures of my MRI. They were too busy going behind my back and researching my family (something they had no right to do), attempting to slap a diagnosis on something they could not see and did not understand. They continued to tell me what they "Think," while I continued to tell them what I "Know" based on my life experiences (Truth).

I asked the doctors if they had read the article from the *Salem News* regarding the silver shekel. Their response was, "Where were you on Holy Thursday in 2006?" which implied that they thought I had planted the shekel there. I replied, "I don't know, probably at school getting ready to leave for Easter weekend." One of the doctors started mentioning my MRI scans. I said, "When you look at the images, tell me what you *see*, not what you *think*." Words cannot express the look of confusion in the doctor's eyes after I had said that. I can recall one of the two doctors offering the comment, "We think you're delusional." I found this to be a typical response from a faithless person who defines himself by his career title. "So the last will be first, and the first last. For many are called, but few chosen" (Matthew 20:16).

Apparently, it's wrong in this day and age for a young man to make positive life changes and become a truthful, helpful person. Another exchanging of words that stands out in my memory was when I told one of the work doctors that I enjoyed helping people; namely through sharing my experiences and hope in the twelve-step program and volunteering at the shelter in my neighborhood. His response, "What if they don't want to be helped?" Wow! I cannot explain how sickening it was to hear another person (namely a doctor) say such a thing. They then told me how they wanted to put me into some hospital. I thought, *Really, for feeling good?!* Again, I'll refer to the Scriptures: "Those who are well have no need of a physician, but those who are sick" (Luke 5:31). Obviously, most people can't understand how a person can be joyful, happy, and positive without chemicals. I hope that you, dear reader, are beginning to understand how it is possible. After one of the doctors mentioned he wanted to put me into some hospital—so I could be away from my fiancée and lay around in a bed—I simply looked him in the eyes and said, "No thank you, I would like to get back to work now if that's okay." I humbly stood up and exited the office. As I was leaving, feeling quite disheartened, I could hear them continue to speak against me and gossip behind my back. This was another doctor's appointment that got me nowhere. I exited the medical center and went back to continue performing my duties on the job.

About a week or so later, November 30, I was scheduled to visit the work doctor again to review the images from my MRI. I was working the night shift (11 p.m.-7 a.m.) at the time, so my appointment was for 7:30 a.m. As I was waiting outside the medical center office at work, I was listening to some Christmas music and enjoying a nice spiritual buzz. I happened to look up into the clouds and I had a vision. I saw a cloud formation that shifted into what looked like an old wise man. As I continued to watch this, there was some light in the cloud formation that looked like a hand waving at me. I then looked off to the right of this, and there was another cloud formation that was in the shape of a perfect cross. I thought, *Wow! I wonder if anyone else is seeing this!* That, I do not know, but I do know what I was seeing.

Shortly after having this vision, I entered the medical center office to check in for my appointment. The doctor was late due to car trouble. I decided to take a walk and grab a quick breakfast and patiently await the doctor's arrival. I returned to the office and continued to wait. Once the doctor finally arrived, he came into the waiting room I was in. He then explained that he was late because he had experienced two flat tires on his way into work. I thought to myself, *It seems like the Good Shepherd is judging him righteously for persecuting and lying to an honest man.*

The doctor then explained that he still had not looked at the images of my MRI. I was somewhat upset for having more of my time wasted, although I really was not surprised.

I then asked him honestly, "Doctor, who gave you permission to research my brother and my family?" He said, "You signed a piece of paper that said we could contact your PCP." I said, "Yes, I signed that paper so you could contact my PCP about me, not my family." The doctor proceeded to stumble over his own words. I said, "So correct me if I'm wrong, sir, but you lied to me. You have gone behind my back unlawfully, without my consent, and you have lied to me." Again, words cannot express the look of confusion in the doctor's eyes. I honestly felt sorry for him. I'm sure that with the career title of doctor, he was used to having people agree with whatever he said.

I then asked him if he could at least explain to me why my hearing had improved so greatly over the past year. The doctor proceeded to throw out big terms and buzz words, yet no simple, logical explanation. (I know how that works, being an engineer and having done some consulting work; I am familiar with throwing out big technical terms to impress clients, etc.) Next, he showed me a picture of the human ear and all the little parts thereof. I calmly asked him, "Doctor, who named all of the parts to the human ear?" He proceeded to tell me how groups of men got together centuries ago and decided what they were to be called. I calmly said to him, "No Doctor, God named those. He works through people. God told those people what the proper identifications were to be for the parts of the ear, as well as all the parts of the human body; and He did it by placing the thoughts in their heads." Once I finished speaking, the look of sheer terror and confusion in the doctor's eyes was astounding; again I felt very sorry for him.

Prior to my leaving his office, I asked the doctor what happened on his way to work. He told me that he experienced two random flat tires, and he only had one spare, which was why he was late; he said it had ruined his day. He then told me he was going to look at the images of my MRI right away and asked if I could come back in a few hours. I told him I was on the night shift and I needed to go home and get some rest. We then agreed that I would come back the following week for another appointment to discuss the results from my MRI. Following this agreement, I left the medical center office at work and headed home to get some sleep.

During that same day, only hours later, I got a phone call from the doctor. I did not answer the call, because I was sleeping. More phone calls followed, and since it was disturbing my peace and my rest, I decided it best to return the call. When I returned the phone call, a woman answered whom I had never met nor spoken to, and she asked, "Is this Michael?" I said, "Yes, it is." She then proceeded to tell me that I was no longer allowed on work property because I was considered a danger to myself and to other people. I was stunned, baffled, confused, insulted, and shocked all at the same time. I asked why, and the answer I received was, "The doctor *thinks* you are mentally disabled." What a blow that was to a young man who had invested four years to earn his bachelor's degree, as well as more time and money invested to earn the proper state licenses and certificates for his own life, well-being, and future. I replied, "Well, okay then." I really had no idea that telling the truth and being honest would enable a doctor to pass so much unrighteous judgment on a person. Nonetheless, since then I have been doing my best to make a negative situation positive.

The situations from the month of November have taught me many valuable life lessons. To begin, I must state clearly that I have zero regrets, nor will I ever regret speaking truthfully (based on my life experiences). Telling the truth is not something I will apologize for. What made me feel disheartened, particularly in this situation, was my supervisor. I shared a great deal of knowledge and wisdom with him, and it truly seemed as though he was listening. Unfortunately, once the doctors got a hold of him and convinced him not to listen to me, he became very doubtful. This experience reminds me of the parable of the sower:

Therefore hear the parable of the sower: "When anyone hears the word of the kingdom, and does not understand it, then the wicked one comes and snatches away what was sown in his heart. This is he who received seed by the wayside. But he who received the seed on stony places, this is he who hears the word and immediately receives it with joy; yet he has no root in himself, but endures only for a while. For when tribulation or persecution arises because of the word, immediately he stumbles. Now he who received seed among the thorns is he who hears the word, and the cares of this world and the deceitfulness of riches choke the word, and he becomes unfruitful. But he who received seed on the good ground is he who hears the word and understands it, who indeed bears fruit and produces: some a hundredfold, some sixty, some thirty." (Matthew 13:18-23)

My supervisor reminds me of one who received the seed on stony places because he was very intrigued and joyful to hear the Word until the doctors (men who define themselves based on a career title; those who are deceived by the riches of this world) caused him to doubt, stumble, and disbelieve. Prior to my last day on the job, I can recall my supervisor saying to me, "Well, if that's what you *believe*." My answer to this statement would be, "No, it is not what I *believe*, it is what I *know*, based on my life experiences (Truth)."

As I have continued to grow on my journey of faith, I came across another spiritual author (Beth Moore) who has had an experience strikingly similar to mine: The author writes,

I remember sharing with a loved one how I know Christ is alive. He said, "I believe in reincarnation," and, "I believe a spiritual presence exists rather than a certain God." He continued by repeating the words "I believe" over and over. Suddenly God gave me such a strange insight, and I was overwhelmed at the difference between my loved one and me. He believed the things he had been taught through New Age philosophy. I didn't just believe. *I knew*. I gently said to him, "My God is not just Someone I believe in. He's Someone I know. I've felt His presence. I've seen His activity. I've experienced His deliverance. I've been touched by His healing. I've witnessed answered prayer. I've 'heard' Him speak straight to me through His Word. Yes, I believe. But more than that, I know."[10]

Wow! (Amen I say to you, Beth.) I read that particular book over a month after my experiences at work, and it brought me peace of mind and joy to know that I am not the only one who has experienced His mighty works. In a matter of absolute truth, I could feel His presence each time I went to speak to the doctors at work, and I know He was with me. This experience reminds me of what Jesus said: "But when they deliver you up, do not worry about how or what you should speak. For it will be given to you in that hour what you should speak; for it is not you who speak, but the Spirit of your Father who speaks in you" (Matthew 10:19-20). "Therefore do not fear them. For there is nothing covered that will not be revealed, and hidden that will not be known" (Matthew 10:26). I did not need to premeditate what I was going to say any time I met with these doctors. As I mentioned earlier, I humbly prayed, "Abba, please speak through me and help me share my experiences with these gentlemen." I am grateful to have Him with me, and I shall not have to regret telling the truth in any given situation.

Some major life lessons from my experiences through the month of November are as follows: I cannot help anyone who is not willing to be helped; I cannot teach anyone who is not willing to be taught; and I cannot save anyone who is not willing to be saved. I have tried to, but it does not work because, unfortunately, some people just do not have the ears to hear, and frankly, some people just don't seem to care about spiritual things, even the destination of their own souls. All I can do is continue to pray for them, continue being faithful and true, and adhere to the teachings of Jesus: "But I say to you, love your enemies, bless those who curse you, do good to those who hate you, and pray for those who spitefully use you and persecute you, that you may be sons of your Father in heaven; for He makes His sun rise on the evil and on the good, and sends rain on the just and on the unjust"(Matthew 5:44-45).

I cannot help but feel sorrowful for these doctors for judging against an innocent, truthful, faithful young man. It reminds me a lot of the following: "Judge not, that you be not judged. For with what judgment you judge, you will be judged; and with the measure you use, it will be measured back to you" (Matthew 7:1-2).

I also relate it to the following:

Do not speak evil of one another, brethren. He who speaks evil of a brother and judges his brother, speaks evil of the law and judges the law. But if you judge the law, you are not a doer of the law but a judge. There is one Lawgiver, who is able to save and to destroy. Who are you to judge another?"(James 4:11-12)

I forgive these doctors for what they have done, but still, I feel remorseful. As they observed me medically, I was observing them spiritually; and each one of them was fast asleep. One thing that really disappointed me about the doctors I spoke with during November was the fact that I asked each one the following simple question, "Why did you become a doctor?" The answer I was looking for was, "To help people." All in all, I have accepted their judgment with grace. It brings me comfort to know that I am not alone. I can relate it also to the teachings of the apostle Paul: "Yes, and all who desire to live godly in Christ Jesus will suffer persecution" (2 Timothy 3:12). Many have come before me who have suffered far greater than I have, so I have no complaints at all for being faithful to my Creator.

More teachings of the apostle Paul which brought me comfort during the month of November are the following:

For the message of the cross is foolishness to those who are perishing, but to us who are being saved it is the power of God. For it is written: "*I will destroy the wisdom of the wise, and bring to nothing the understanding of the prudent.*" [Scripture from Isaiah 29:14] Where is the wise? Where is the scribe? Where is the disputer of this age? Has not God made foolish the wisdom of this world? For since, in the wisdom of God, the world through wisdom did not know God, it pleased God through the foolishness of the message preached to save those who believe . . . . Because the foolishness of God is wiser than men, and the weakness of God is stronger than men." (1 Corinthians 1:18-21, 25)

In touching upon this writing from Paul, I must say that experience has taught me the difference between teaching and preaching. When a person speaks truthfully (based on his/her own life experiences) it is teaching; when a person speaks of events he or she has never experienced, or events yet to come (such as prophecy) it is preaching. November was a month of vast spiritual growth for me; it is a period of time that I shall continue to reflect on with dignity, and I appreciate how God strengthened my soul and enabled me to grow in my faith in Him. "And not only that, but we also glory in tribulations, knowing that tribulation produces perseverance; and perseverance, character; and character, hope. Now hope does not disappoint, because the love of God has been poured out in our hearts by the Holy Spirit who was given to us" (Romans 5:3-5).

DECEMBER

The month of December provided many more opportunities for growth. Through December, I continued to share my experiences through the twelve-step programs; namely speaking at commitments, jails, institutions, and shelters. It brought me joy to share my message of hope with men and women who were willing to listen and receive it. I continued to grow in my faith, one day at a time. I also continued to seek knowledge through spiritual authors and God's Word (the Holy Bible); and most importantly, I continued to seek the Father through prayer. I remained open-minded and continued to listen to the life experiences of others at meetings, commitments, and in everyday life.

I remember feeling very grateful and joyful during the holidays of both Christmas and Hanukkah (my fiancée's father is Jewish) because it felt nice to be able to appreciate the spirit of the season. It was nice to feel the joy of the season for what it really is: a time to be with family, friends, and loved ones; to enjoy each other's company, and celebrate the holidays, namely the birth of the Lord Christ Jesus. I did not have a great deal of money to spend this year, in particular due to the work situation I mentioned from November. This was quite all right with me though, because it enabled me to appreciate the season without having to worry about materialism; I decided I would give time, patience, and love instead. It was also nice to reflect on years past, and to enjoy and appreciate memories of my life and my childhood. All in all, December 2010 was a good month of growth, learning, appreciation, and soul strengthening under the grace of God.

In conclusion to this segment, I would like to note that it has been over a year since the beginning of my journey. I have been back at my place of work since April 2011. I was forced to visit three different health-care professionals, and I was subsequently given medical clearance. I was found able to return to work with zero restrictions by each doctor. It turns out that I am not delusional; however I had to learn the hard way that it is very difficult to talk about faith with people who do not have any. I can say that I feel good every day, and I am continuing to keep the faith.

CHAPTER THREE

Commandments, Golden Rule, Prayers, Finding the Narrow Way, God's Names

THE TEN COMMANDMENTS (EXODUS 20:1-17)

1. I am the LORD your God, who brought you out of the land of Egypt, out of the house of bondage. You shall have no other gods before Me.

2. You shall not make for yourself a carved image—any likeness of anything that is in heaven above, or that is in the earth beneath, or that is in the water under the earth; you shall not bow down to them nor serve them. For I, the LORD your God, am a jealous God, visiting the iniquity of the fathers upon the children to the third and fourth generations of those who hate Me, but showing mercy to thousands, to those who love Me and keep My Commandments.

3. You shall not take the name of the LORD your God in vain, for the LORD will not hold him guiltless who takes His name in vain.

4. Remember the Sabbath day, to keep it holy.

5. Honor your father and your mother, that your days may be long upon the land which the LORD your God is giving you.

6. You shall not murder.

7. You shall not commit adultery.

8. You shall not steal.

9. You shall not bear false witness against your neighbor.

10. You shall not covet your neighbor's house; you shall not covet your neighbor's wife, nor his male servant, nor his female servant, nor his ox, nor his donkey, nor anything that is your neighbor's.

Those are the Ten Commandments from the book of Exodus. I am not a theologian, so I shall let you take what you wish from these. I must say, however, that in growing spiritually I began to realize that they really are a simple guide to living, and they are not too difficult to adhere to. God's laws are not meant to punish me; He just wants me to live a full, positive, and joyful life. God does not want me to have to carry regrets and soul sickness around. I have realized that by following these simple laws, I will not get into trouble with the laws of my country, or city, etc. I am not perfect; if I break a commandment, I ask His forgiveness in prayer.

The Golden Rule

Therefore, whatever you want men to do to you, do also to them, for this is the Law and the Prophets. (Matthew 7:12)

And just as you want men to do to you, you also do to them likewise. (Luke 6:31)

In layman's terms: I treat other people the way I, myself, want to be treated.

Finding the Narrow Way

Enter by the narrow gate; for wide is the gate and broad is the way that leads to destruction, and there are many who go in by it. Because narrow is the gate and difficult is the way which leads to life, and there are few who find it. (Matthew 7:13-14)

Twelve Steps to Finding the Narrow Way

1. I admitted that I am a human being, I am powerless over the sinful ways of human nature, and I want to be a happier, healthier, more loving and joyful person.
2. I came to believe that a power greater than myself could restore me to sanity.
3. I made a decision to turn my life and my will over to the care of God, as I understand Him.
4. I made a searching and fearless moral inventory of myself.
5. I admitted to God, to myself, and to another human being the exact nature of my wrongs.
6. I was entirely ready to have God remove all these defects of character.
7. I humbly asked Him to remove my shortcomings.
8. I made a list of all persons I had harmed, and became willing to make amends to them all.

9. I made direct amends to such people wherever possible, except when to do so would injure them or others.

10. I continue to take personal moral inventory and when I am wrong, promptly admit to it.

11. I seek through prayer and meditation to improve my conscious contact with God, as I understand Him, praying only for knowledge of His will for me and the power to carry that out.

12. Having had a spiritual awakening as the result of these steps, I try to carry a positive message of hope to people wherever I go, and to practice these principles in all my affairs.

SIMPLIFIED:

1. My name is _____, I am a human being (one of the Good Lord's finest and most prized creations), and I want to be a happier, more positive, joyful person so I can appreciate life more.

2. In prayer, from a quiet place: "God, please restore me to sanity."

3. In prayer, from a quiet place: "Spirit of the living God, please enter my body and show me the way which leads to life."

4. With pen and paper ready to write: "God, loving Creator, please help me and guide me to do a thorough moral inventory of my life, so I can better understand myself."

5. Read the moral inventory out loud. You, dear reader, can choose to address it to whoever you want to. (I chose a person that I would not have to see again, because there was some personal stuff in there.)

6. "God, loving Creator, the One who sees me, I thank You from the bottom of my heart that I now know You better. Please forgive me if I have left anything out of my moral inventory, and please help me to grow with You and become the person You created me to be." (Grateful, happy, loving, joyful, appreciative, etc.)

7. "God, please remove my shortcomings so that I may continue to grow with You."

8. In my step 8, I took my moral inventory and underlined any of the names that came up. I made my list of these names.

9. I made amends to these people, some using e-mail, some using the phone, some I had already made amends to in the past. I made sure to only mention how I was sorry, not placing any blame on them, because my step work was to clear my conscience and free my soul.

10. I simply keep a journal of sorts to keep track of myself, and my life. *You, dear reader, should be the most important person in your life. Your life is important; do not let anyone tell you otherwise.*

11. I personally find that negative thoughts and emotions are no match when I involve prayer. I pray in my head sometimes, but when I do my morning prayers, I pray out loud; usually just a whisper. God is always listening, and He wants me to be a happy, loving person; He did not create me to be hateful and miserable.

12. Very simple: living the Golden Rule. Treating others the way I, myself, want to be treated. If they do not appreciate my kindness, that is their problem, not mine.

PRINCIPLES OF A TWELVE-STEP PROGRAM

Experience, Strength, and Hope: When a person speaks of life experiences, that person is telling the truth. I realize that I only know something to be true if I have experienced it in my life.

And you shall know the truth, and the truth shall make you free. (John 8:32)

Jesus said to him, "I am the way, the truth, and the life. No one comes to the Father except through Me." (John 14:6)
Sanctify them by Your truth. Your word is truth. (John 17:17)

"Everyone who is of the truth hears My voice. (John 18:37)

52

Keep It Simple: Don't overwhelm yourself; nobody can retransform his/her entire life in one day. Some of the greatest ideas throughout the course of history have been very simple ideas. For example: the wheel.

Live in the Day and Do the Next Right Thing: It is okay to plan for the future (vacations, schooling, etc.), but I find it important to fully enjoy and make each day count. In my experiences, I realized I was rushing right through life and constantly living for the *next____*, and I missed out on a great deal of the present time. Doing the next right thing can be the simple things: holding the door for someone, saying please and thank you, asking a person if they need help (if they say no, well at least you've offered). It is simply learning to enjoy the realness and beauty of each day of life.

People, Places, and Things: I had to learn to stay away from anything negative. I began involving myself with positive people, places, and things.

Live and Let Live: I cannot expect anyone else to know as I know, or think the same way as I do. If everyone looked the same and spoke the same language, the world would be a pretty boring place. It is coming to understand the simple dignity of difference, and living the Golden Rule.

Easy Does It: I had to learn to be easier on myself. Also I had to learn to not hate myself, to avoid speaking against and insulting myself, and to start to become a more positive person one day at a time.

Very Important: You, dear reader, must make the decision to pursue a life of truth and honesty prior to beginning the step work. I would personally recommend being free of mind-altering chemical substances (drugs and alcohol) for starters, because in my experience it was chemicals that were keeping me out of the Light. It won't be easy at first, but it will become easier with each passing day. It helped me in the beginning to simply ask God to remove the desire with my morning prayer. If you, dear reader, don't want to call Him God, you can simply call Him Life; I do hope you believe in life. For example: "Good morning, Life, thank you for this new day. Please help me to stay sober and be a positive person, just for today." Then at night before bed, "Thank you, Life, for a good day." It really is that simple. I know, I have lived it and experienced it. It seems hard to believe at first, but I know from experience that a spiritual high is far more exhilarating than any man-made chemical high.

There came a point in my life when I started asking myself some deep questions. Who am I? Why am I here? What is the meaning to all this? I felt as if I were lost. I decided to take a huge leap of faith and began seeking God and making a conscious effort to start living an honest life. I realized that most ideas are simple, and life really can be simple as long as I don't complicate it for myself. Once I sincerely took this type of position and began putting God first (starting each day with a quick prayer), many miracles began to happen. I had a brand-new start and a new perspective on life. I began to realize how powerful God really is, and He provides everything I need as long as I keep close to Him with a willingness to grow in His image one day at a time. Once these wonderful changes began to manifest in my life, I became less and less interested in myself and my little plans, and I became interested with what I could contribute to life. In doing so, I began to feel more power and Spirit flow in, which brought peace of mind, serenity, and awareness unlike I had previously known. I began to discover that I can face life successfully, and as I became more conscious of His presence, my fear of today, tomorrow, and the hereafter began to disappear—I felt completely reborn.

PRAYERS

Here are some prayers I learned and started saying during the beginning of my journey. As I grew spiritually I began to develop a better understanding of these prayers. I find these particular prayers, when said with sincerity, have really worked for me. As I grew spiritually in recovery, I began to notice how the principles of the program seemed to provide further insight into the prayers.

Serenity Prayer
God, grant me the serenity to accept the things I cannot change, the courage to change the things I can, and the wisdom to know the difference.

Serenity Prayer (long version)
God, grant me the serenity to accept the things I cannot change, courage to change the things I can, and the wisdom to know the difference. Living one day at a time; enjoying one moment at a time; accepting hardship as the pathway to peace. Taking, as He did, this sinful world as it is, not as I would have it. Trusting that He will make things right if I surrender to His will; that I may be reasonably happy in this life, and supremely happy with Him forever in the next. Amen

Lord's Prayer
Our Father
Who art in heaven
Hallowed be Thy name
Thy kingdom come, Thy will be done, on earth as it is in heaven
Give us this day our daily bread
And forgive us our trespasses

As we forgive those who trespass against us
And lead us not into temptation
But deliver us from evil
For Thine is the kingdom, the power, and the glory, forever.
Amen

NAMES OF THE SPIRIT OF GOD ALMIGHTY[1]

-ELOHIM
-ADONAI
-JEHOVA-YAHWEH
-JEHOVA-
  MACCADDESHEM
-JEHOVA-ROHI
-JEHOVA-SHAMMAH
-JEHOVA-RAPHA
-JEHOVA-TSIDKENU
-JEHOVA-NISSI
-JEHOVA-SHALOM
-JEHOVA-SADDAOTH
-JEHOVA-GMOLAH
-EL-ELYON
-EL-ROI
-EL-SHADDAI
-EL-OLAM
-ABBA
-ADVOCATE
-ALMIGHTY
-ALPHA
-AMEN
-ANCIENT OF DAYS
-ANOINTED ONE
-APOSTLE
-ARM OF THE LORD
-AUTHOR OF LIFE
-AUTHOR OF OUR
  FAITH
-BEGINNING
-BLESSED HOLY
  RULER
-BRANCH

-BREAD OF GOD
-BREAD OF LIFE
-BRIDE GROOM
-BRIGHT MORNING
  STAR
-CHIEF SHEPHERD
-CHOSEN ONE
-CHRIST
-CHRIST OF GOD
-CHRIST THE LORD
-CHRIST, SON OF
  LIVING GOD
-COMFORTER
-COMMANDER
-CONSOLATION OF
  ISRAEL
-CONSUMING FIRE
-CORNERSTONE
-COUNSELOR
-CREATOR
-DELIVERER
-DESIRED OF ALL
  NATIONS
-DOOR
-END
-ETERNAL GOD
-EVERLASTING
  FATHER
-FAITHFUL & TRUE
-FAITHFUL WITNESS
-FATHER
-FIRSTBORN
-FIRSTFRUITS

-FOUNDATION
-FRIEND OF TAX
  COLLECTORS &
  SINNERS
-GENTLE WHISPERER
-GIFT OF GOD
-GLORY OF THE
  LORD
-GOD
-GOD ALMIGHTY
-GOD OVER ALL
-GOD WHO SEES ME
-GOOD SHEPHERD
-GUIDE
-HEAD OF THE BODY
-HEAD OF THE
  CHURCH
-HEIR OF ALL
  THINGS
-HIGH PRIEST
-HOLY ONE
-HOLY ONE OF
  ISRAEL
-HOLY SPIRIT
-HOPE
-HORN OF
  SALVATION
-I AM
-IMAGE OF GOD
-IMAGE OF HIS
  PERSON
-IMMANUEL
-JEALOUS

-JEHOVA
-JESUS
-JESUS CHRIST OUR
  LORD
-JUDGE
-KING
-KING ETERNAL
-KING OF KINGS
-KING OF THE AGES
-LAMB OF GOD
-LAST ADAM
-LAW GIVER
-LEADER
-LIFE
-LIGHT OF THE
  WORLD
-LIKE AN EAGLE
-LILY OF THE
  VALLEYS
-LION OF THE TRIBE
  OF JUDAH
-LIVING STONE
-LIVING WATER
-LORD
-LORD GOD
  ALMIGHTY
-LORD JESUS CHRIST
-LORD OF ALL
-LORD OF GLORY
-LORD OF HOSTS
-LORD OF LORDS
-LORD OF
  RIGHTEOUSNESS
-LOVE
-MAN OF SORROWS

-MASTER
-MERCIFUL GOD
-MESSENGER OF THE
  COVENANT
-MESSIAH
-MIGHTY GOD
-MIGHTY ONE
-NAZARENE
-OFFSPRING OF
  DAVID
-OMEGA
-ONLY BEGOTTEN
  SON
-OUR PASSOVER
  LAMB
-OUR PEACE
-POTTER
-POWER OF GOD
-PRINCE OF PEACE
-PROPHET
-PURIFIER
-RABBONI
  (TEACHER)
-RADIANCE OF GOD'S
  GLORY
-REDEEMER
-REFINER'S FIRE
-RESURRECTION
-RIGHTEOUS ONE
-ROCK
-ROOT OF DAVID
-ROSE OF SHARON
-RULER OF GOD'S
  CREATION

-RULER OVER KINGS
  OF EARTH
-RULER OVER ISRAEL
-SAVIOR
-SCEPTER OUT OF
  ISRAEL
-SEED
-SERVANT
-SHEPHERD OF OUR
  SOULS
-SHIELD
-SON OF DAVID
-SON OF GOD
-SON OF MAN
-SON OF THE MOST
  HIGH
-SOURCE
-SPIRIT OF GOD
-STAR OUT OF JACOB
-STONE
-SUN OF
  RIGHTEOUSNESS
-TEACHER
-TRUE LIGHT
-TRUE WITNESS
-TRUTH
-VINE
-WAY
-WISDOM OF GOD
-WITNESS
-WONDERFUL
-WORD
-WORD OF GOD

CHAPTER FOUR

In Depth with the
Spirit of the Universe

In Depth with My Experiences

In this chapter, dear reader, I shall take you a little further into the spiritual realm, based upon my life experiences. As I mentioned, in the month of September 2010, I saw the sixes (666) everywhere (license plates, receipts, etc.). I also had dreams of battles of good versus evil. These dreams included demons and devilish-looking people, and I will admit that this was quite scary at first, but I could tell I was starting to follow the right path. I remember having negativity come at me from all sides.

It was mid-September, and one of my neighbors had the habit of leaving his television on full volume through all hours of the night. It was difficult for my fiancée and me to sleep. I wrote him a note kindly asking him to turn the volume down. As I recall, this happened on two or three occasions. One afternoon, my neighbor came knocking on my door and was acting very confrontational. He said, "I understand about the volume, but you didn't have to rip my apartment number off the wall and throw it down the hallway!" I told him that I had nothing to do with that. I kept my cool, remained impeccable with my word (speaking truthfully), and told him that if he continued to have problems with vandalizing I suggested that he take it up with management. I know I had nothing to do with the mysterious defacing of his property of which he was complaining. I reassured him that my fiancée and I were peaceful people, and all we had done was place a note under his door on two separate occasions. It was not easy to respond without giving in to the temptation of argument, but God's grace enabled me to maintain my composure.

Another instance occurred while I was at work. This time, an old girlfriend of mine sent me a random text message. I could tell, based on the hour of the night, that she had most likely been drinking. I was tempted to respond and ask her how she was doing, but I did not. I remained impeccable with my word and responded, "I don't think your new boyfriend would appreciate you texting me, and I am quite certain my girlfriend would not appreciate it." That was the end of that; simple, but truthful and honest. I could tell that I was being tempted, so I found a quiet place, knelt down, and prayed, "Father, I can see that I am being tempted, please help me to be strong and do right in Your eyes always." That simple prayer enabled me to be strong and relax.

On another occasion, two of the light bulbs in the corridor of my apartment building burst at random during the night. I could sense that something dark was very unhappy because I was waking from the spiritual sleep.

In September I decided to call my friend Bill, whom I had met in the two-week program, to thank him for his positive guidance. I remember the phone call very well. I thanked him for giving me the copy of his book from the twelve-step program[1] and for helping me get started on my journey. I can remember him saying, "You know Mike, I hadn't read that book in years, but the thought just came to me that I should bring it with me to the program." We shared a few positive experiences, and that was that. I could feel the presence of the Holy Spirit even as we spoke over the phone. I knew God had put the thought in his head to bring the book with him, because God already knew in advance that I would need it.

Also in September, more positive memories started coming back to me. I remembered being a little fat kid in elementary school. I recalled, at some point in my youth, looking in the mirror of my bedroom, and I had a vision of how I wanted to look when I got older. I then remembered an instance from sophomore year in high school when I was washing my hands in the boy's bathroom and I looked in the mirror. I thought, *My God, is that really what I look like?* I now understand that God had been molding me into the person I hoped to be.

I remembered one particular football practice from my freshman year of high school. After practice, while we were throwing the ball around, I said out loud, "I will be the quarterback of this football team senior year." People laughed, because I wasn't politically connected and I was a chunky defensive lineman at the time. I also remembered a writing assignment from English class that same year. The teacher told us to write this assignment from the perspective of a graduating senior looking back at our high school experiences. I can recall the teacher said, "Feel free to toot your own horn." Well, I decided to write that essay and I did toot my own horn. I wrote about quarterbacking the football team to the Super Bowl. Again, I wrote this essay freshman year.

Sophomore year, for some reason or other, I decided not to play football. During the winter of my sophomore year, I remember the football coach, Steve Hayden—a very positive, kind, faithful man—approached me and convinced me to go out for the team. Based on his positive advice, I went out for the team junior year. I recall beginning the season as a tight end, which I was happy with because I had good hands and I figured I would at least get to touch the ball on occasion. Unfortunately, during the second day of training camp, the coach approached me and said, "Mike, you're a big kid; I think we are going to move you to center." I'll admit I was somewhat disappointed, but I did what I was told.

Through the first month of that season, I remember feeling unmotivated. I continued to pay attention to the quarterbacks, how they ran the plays and their footwork, etc. One day at practice (I believe it was early October 2000) one of the scout team quarterbacks was struggling with his passing. The coach asked if anyone there could throw a football, and I responded with, "Yeah Coach, I can throw a little bit." I ran some plays on the practice team and did my best to emulate the motions of the starting quarterback. The following day I was coming out of cooking class, and the coach was waiting for me in the hallway. I instantly thought, *Oh no, I'm in trouble.* What the coach said to me was, "Mike, I'd like you to learn quarterback." My first thought was, *Wow, is this really happening!?* I remember the coach shaking my hand and looking me right in the eye as if to say, "Wake up donkey! I'm trying to give you your dream!" I learned the position and played quarterback for the practice squad for the remainder of junior year. This gave me a great opportunity for growth because our football team had one of the top defenses in the state.

In my senior year, I began the season as the backup quarterback. Through some strange coincidences, I got to start the fourth game into the season and continued to start every game for the remainder of that season. I kept it simple and did the best I could to help the team. The team ended up winning the league championship that year, and we went to the Super Bowl. We did not win the Super Bowl, but I guess you can't win them all. In truth, freshman year I did not write about winning the Super Bowl, I just wrote that we went to the Super Bowl. I can remember taking a knee before each game, putting my fist to the ground, and praying, "God please grant me the strength to do the best I can to help the team." I remember hearing this little voice click in my head saying, *You've got it!*

I can remember playing in big games, but not feeling too nervous about it; I felt confidence, poise, and a relaxed focus. I remember throwing passes to perfection—what felt like out-of-body experiences. One time, after a fifty-yard touchdown pass, I came off the field and asked one of the coaches, "Did I really just throw that?" He said, "Michael, you've got a great arm!" I did have a great arm, but I now understand that it was the Spirit working through me. The truth is, it was my dream to play quarterback. It took some hard work and paying attention on my part, as well as the faith of my coach to show me the way so I could live the life I imagined. In my college football career when I got away from praying before games, my performance and level of poise suffered for it because I thought I had been doing it all on my own. My record as a starter in college suffered immensely for my foolishness.

More memories which returned to me in September 2010 were from my career in baseball. I could remember being a little boy, and my dad would take me to the field to teach me how to catch, throw, and hit. After a couple of years, my dad saw that I had some ability and talent. The truth is he had taken me as far as he could. He then decided it was best to bring me to a baseball camp which was directed by one of his high school friends, coach Frank Carey (Coach Carey has over 650 wins with North Reading High School in Massachusetts). I learned a great deal about baseball at this camp, and I learned the position of catcher. From a young age, as a little fat kid, my dream was to be the varsity catcher of my high school baseball team. Through some hard work and paying attention, I was able to develop my skills based on the coaching of the elite at this camp. There were coaches there from all over the United States, and these coaches had produced many professional athletes. As the years passed, I attended this camp each summer and continued to grow and develop.

In spite of some negative coaching at my own high school, I was able to achieve my dream of being the varsity catcher. It seemed as if some of the coaches at my high school were not happy that I had received my coaching from a different school in the area. One memory stands out in particular: it was senior year in high school (spring 2002), and one of my friends had a bunch of people over on Good Friday and there was drinking involved. I stopped by this party, but I did not have any drinks because I was planning to go to church with my mom. The police showed up and busted everyone for under-age drinking. I told them I hadn't been drinking, had a brief conversation with one of the officers, and he let me leave. I then went about my day and went to church with my mom that afternoon.

The following week, the athletic director and the varsity baseball coach brought me in for questioning regarding the party on Good Friday. The director stated, "If you drank, you can just tell us; we will suspend you for a couple of games, but it's no big deal." I said, "I did not drink." He said, "If you had a couple of beers, you can just tell us." I told him "I did not have any beers; and in truth, if I did drink it would not have been just a couple, it would have been more like seven or eight—but I did not have any." It seemed as if the coach and the athletic director were disappointed, because they wanted to suspend me. Nonetheless, I simply told the truth and was not suspended. The truth is that I wanted to be the varsity catcher of my baseball team. The way for me to accomplish this goal was through hard work, attentiveness, and good coaching, so I could live the life I imagined.

As I grew throughout September, I started to become more patient. I was actually able to communicate with a neighbor of mine, who is a deaf man. All it required was a little patience, a pen, and some paper. This was something I never would have thought possible in my old way of living because I would have most likely found an excuse as to why I was too busy for him. The grace of God has enabled me to be more patient and understanding, and I now communicate with this man on a regular basis by simply speaking slowly, and listening intently when he speaks.

As I fore mentioned, I bought my girlfriend an engagement ring in the latter half of September. I began shopping with her friend in the middle of that month. I made a quick purchase one afternoon and was eager to pop the question. Her friend called me later that same evening and said, "You know, Mike, it's a beautiful ring, but I think we can do better." I agreed with hesitation. I'll admit I was somewhat disappointed; however, I realized that I was being selfish. This was not about me, it was about my girlfriend. I realized that an engagement ring is a one-shot deal and I should get it right the first time.

Her friend and I did a little more shopping around and found the perfect ring. Next, I needed to come up with the money. I decided to borrow some of my own money from my retirement savings (I can't guarantee that I'm going to live to the age of sixty-five), so I could use my own money for the purchase. While at work on a Wednesday, I filled out the loan application. The money was to arrive in seven to ten business days. That evening, I went to a quiet place and prayed, "Father, I know You put this young woman in my life for a reason. I would like to ask her to marry me next Friday. If there is anything You can do to help the money arrive as quickly as possible, I would greatly appreciate it." I received the check in the mail two days later. Some would call this a coincidence, but in my understanding, it was the handiwork of God.

As I revealed earlier, I purchased a pendant of Michael the Archangel in the beginning of September. I can remember certain occasions at work when negative memories and negative emotions would start to creep up on me. These were feelings of uncertainty and insecurity, or even anxiety. Without thinking, I would take hold of the Archangel pendant and whisper, "Saint Michael, kindly smash this demon back to the depths where it belongs." Upon saying this, I would shut my eyes and envision a bolt of lightning. When I opened my eyes, I felt pure serenity and inner peace. The negative emotion was eliminated. I began calling on the Archangel Michael whenever any negative memory or emotion would try to rear its ugly head. In case you don't know about the Archangel Michael, dear reader, he is viewed as the field commander of the Army of God. He is very powerful, and he has always helped me whenever I've asked him to intervene on the Lord's behalf.

There were days in September when it felt as if I were walking on air. I remember one evening at work when hymns started coming to me. One in particular that stands out is "Holy Holy Holy (Hosanna)": "Holy, holy, holy Lord. God of Power God of might. Heaven and Earth are full of Your glory. Hosanna in the Highest. Blessed is He who comes in the name of the Lord."[2]

I remember thinking, *Wow!* I could remember those songs from childhood. I wasn't really an avid churchgoer, except on holidays or other special occasions, but I didn't quite understand why these hymns were coming to me so suddenly. I figured I would continue walking the path I was now on, because it seemed as if I were headed in the right direction. It was somewhat overwhelming, but it felt great to be on such a spiritual high. I wished everyone could have felt that way.

I mentioned earlier, dear reader, that I had been having some bad dreams early-on in September. Towards the end of that month, however, I began to have good dreams. They were dreams and visions of Jesus of Nazareth (the Christ). I had dreams of how Jesus prayed, how He taught people, and how He helped people. I remember one dream in particular of Jesus praying from His knees, with the white light of the Holy Spirit shining onto His head. I followed those dreams and began praying in a similar fashion. I continued to have dreams of Jesus praying with His hands open and cupped:

> But this is what was spoken by the prophet Joel: *"And it shall come to pass in the last days, says God, that I will pour out My Spirit on all flesh; your sons and your daughters shall prophesy, your young men shall see visions, your old men shall dream dreams. And on My menservants and on My maidservants I will pour out My Spirit in those days; and they shall prophesy. I will show wonders in heaven above and signs on the earth beneath: blood and fire and vapor of smoke. The sun shall be turned into darkness, and the moon into blood, before the coming of the great and awesome day of the LORD. And it shall come to pass that whoever calls on the name of the LORD shall be saved."* [Joel 2:28-32] (Acts 2:16-21)

I could not discern what this particular dream meant, but I figured it out eventually, which I will tell you later in this chapter.

Something very amazing happened to me on the night of September 23. That night I was working the 11 p.m. to 7 a.m. shift. I was experiencing some awesome spiritual highs, and I felt incredible. During this point in my journey, I had yet to finish my moral inventory. I was standing near my work post, and I thought, *I wonder if anyone has ever thoroughly followed these twelve steps?* I then heard this voice in my head, a very powerful and positive voice, and it said, *Michael, if you do this for Me, this is what I shall give you.* At that instant, my brain was hit with a blast of dopamine. It was the highest feeling I have ever experienced. I thought, *Wow! What exactly does this mean?* I wasn't sure what was happening at the time, but I figured I'd enjoy the buzz. I couldn't sit still, I felt so amazing, so alive. I just thought, *Wow, I don't know what this means, but I guess for now I'll just keep it simple; live in the day and do the next right thing.* I wasn't sure about this voice, but it was very positive, and I had never experienced such a high feeling before.

At this point, I had read just about every piece of literature from the twelve-step program that I could get my hands on. With all of the memories that were coming back to me, I felt somewhat overwhelmed, so I decided I would try reading the literature again. One evening, as I began to do this, a voice in my head said, *Michael, you have come this way already. I would like you to continue to grow with Me.* I figured it was time to read the pastor's book that I had purchased prior to the two-week program.

I decided to read *What in the World Is Going On?* by Dr. David Jeremiah.[3] The pastor's book also lead me to read the book of Revelation. I've gained a great deal of insight from this book. One Scripture from Revelation jumped out at me: "Do not fear any of those things which you are about to suffer. Indeed, the devil is about to throw some of you into prison, that you may be tested, and you will have tribulation ten days. Be faithful until death, and I will give you the crown of life" (Revelation 2:10). I was amazed by this, due to the fact that I had a spiritual awakening ten days into the two-week program which I attended.

In truth, before this point, I had gone through two trials. At the first trial, I had a fair judge who was actually willing to hear the case before making a judgment, and he proclaimed a mistrial. At the second trial, I had to plead out because the judge made his judgment before even hearing the case and wanted to put me in jail. I thought of the judge I had in court for my second trial; a man who wanted to throw me into prison prior to hearing my case, regardless of my bachelor's degree, my job, my family, and my life. A man who had prejudged me and had no clue that I was not a bad person—I just needed to be informed that I had a problem and there was a way to fix that problem in order to make a positive life change.

Naturally, in today's world, it makes more sense to ruin a person's life than to help a person to make positive changes to have a better life. This judge was very ready, as he even told my lawyer, to put me in jail based on his prejudgment. A judge full of pride, ego, and self-righteousness; a man who puts on the robe and thinks he can play God. Using the simple numbers of prophesy (where A=1, B=2, C=3, etc.) I was able to decipher that the name of this judge equaled 667. Somewhat like the devil, dressed up in the body of a man, who would have thrown me in jail had I not plead out and taken the two-week program in which I received the crown of life after ten days. Coincidence? I'll let you, dear reader, be the judge of that.

As I worked on my moral inventory (or if you prefer, my confession) during the month of September, certain quotes and realizations came to me from the Holy Spirit. Some are listed here:

When intending to pass judgment, one should walk over to a mirror, gaze deep into his/her own eyes, and begin the process of passing judgment there.

Man is unable to feel or experience true love, until he truly loves and understands himself.
It has become quite clear to me that everything that has happened in my life up to this point has happened for a reason. It is those reasons that I am just now beginning to understand.

I have come to the realization that everything I thought would happen in this life has happened, be it for the positive or the negative.

September 29, 2010 (thirty-six days into my journey): *Positive thoughts come from God—Goodness, Love, Light, Truth, Salvation.*

Negative thoughts come from Evil—Meanness, Cruelty, Corruption, Darkness, Doom, Hatred.

I remember sharing all of these realizations with an adviser and him saying, "Wow! Have you shared this stuff with a priest or anything?" In truth, I tried to share it with the Catholic priest when I sat down for my fifth step (confession), but even he did not understand. I could tell that the priest had never felt the presence of the Holy Spirit. It makes me sad to see a man give up his God-given right to marry and procreate. As I mentioned in chapter 2 the priest seemed more interested in my sex life than my repentance. I wanted to tell him that he should have become a pastor, that way he could have been married and still served God. Days after my confession, I realized that in the Catholic religion, people are worshipping a symbol of wood and a carved image:

"You shall not make for yourself a carved image—any likeness of anything that is in heaven above, or that is in the earth beneath, or that is in the water under the earth; you shall not bow down to them nor serve them. For I, the LORD your God, am a jealous God, visiting the iniquity of the fathers upon the children to the third and fourth generations of those who hate Me, but showing mercy to thousands, to those who love Me and keep My commandments." (Exodus 20:4-6)

And without controversy great is the mystery of godliness: God was manifested in the flesh, justified in the Spirit, seen by angels, preached among the Gentiles, believed on in the world, received up in glory.

Now the Spirit expressly says that in latter times some will depart from the faith, giving heed to deceiving spirits and doctrines of demons, speaking lies in hypocrisy, having their own conscience seared with a hot iron, forbidding to marry, and commanding to abstain from foods which God created to be received with thanksgiving by those who believe and know the truth. For every creature of God is good, and nothing is to be refused if it is received with thanksgiving; for it is sanctified by the word of God and prayer." (1 Timothy 3:16-4:5)

I felt very sorry that this man had fallen for a false prophet and given so much time and so much of his life to it. From Jesus of Nazareth:

Not everyone who says to Me, "Lord, Lord," shall enter the kingdom of heaven, but he who does the will of My Father in heaven. Many will say to Me in that day, "Lord, Lord, have we not prophesied in Your name, cast out demons in Your name, and done many wonders in Your name?" And then I will declare to them, "I never knew you; depart from Me, you who practice lawlessness!" (Matthew 7:21-23)

I have also noticed that often times the Catholic religion promotes hatred (namely towards Jewish people), and in my experience it is rare to meet a Catholic who is very open-minded and accepting. On the contrary, the good, kind, peaceful Catholic who loves God and is a kindhearted person who does not hate or judge another person for his/her differences, he/she is still a child of God. It just makes me sad to see a person bow to idols. One thing I can remember from going to Catholic mass as a child is the following: "Lord, I am not worthy to receive You, but only say the word and I shall be healed." This prayer sounds like spiritual poison to me; this prayer will surely keep a person away from God. In my understanding, it should say, "Lord, please help me to be worthy to receive You. Giver of life, please enter my body and please heal me!" As the Scripture says, "O LORD my God, I cried out to You, and You healed me. O LORD, You brought my soul up from the grave; You have kept me alive, that I should not go down to the pit" (Psalm 30:2-3).

It makes me sad to see how many people have chosen to become atheists because negative experiences with religion turned them away from faith in God. I understand that the twelve steps are about faith, not religion; just as God, as I understand Him, is about faith, not religion. As I understand it, Judaism is a faith based upon the teachings of Moses and the prophets, and Christianity is a faith based on the teachings of Christ and His apostles. Faith is God-made, religion is man-made. God and faith in Him shall have me healed from the inside out, while it seems that religion promotes change from the outside in. As I previously mentioned, I have a relationship with God, not a religion.

I can recall an instance when I was at a morning meeting early in October. I tried to share some of the knowledge that was being given to me from the Spirit with one of the women at this particular meeting because I could tell that she was a spiritual person. I said, "There is a lot happening in my life that seems to make a lot of sense, but I could use some guidance." She said, "Talk to Phil, he's been in the program for nearly fifty years." I approached this man and said, "My name is Michael. I was born of the flesh in February of 1984; I was born of the Spirit in August of 2010." His initial response was, "Never mind that nonsense." I then tried to show him some of my writings, but he immediately cut me off and began speaking over me. As he was talking, this voice again spoke to me through my conscience and said, *Michael, do not listen to this man; this man does not know as you know.* So I let Phil finish speaking and politely thanked him—then I continued walking in the light. I began to understand that the voice I was hearing in my head was God's voice; He was protecting me from falseness and confusion, and He was guiding me in the right direction. As I continued to grow in faith and walk away from the negative ways of my past, I felt more spiritual on the inside and I witnessed my prayers being answered.

I find it amazingly helpful to start my day with a prayer in my quiet place (my bathroom), and end my day with a prayer. I find that it gives me great peace of mind to pray in quiet places whenever I am in need of strength and guidance:

"But you, when you pray, go into your room, and when you have shut your door, pray to your Father who is in the secret place;

and your Father who sees in secret will reward you openly. And when you pray, do not use vain repetitions as the heathen do. For they think that they will be heard for their many words. Therefore do not be like them. For your Father knows the things you have need of before you ask Him." (Matthew 6:6-8)

Nonetheless, one day in the latter half of October, I was praying in my bathroom (I try not to premeditate my prayers; I just pray from the heart) and I was thanking God for my life and all that He has given me and done for me in my life. I can remember these words just coming out of my mouth, "Wow Father, You truly are an awesome God, the God of gods. You've given me the life of my dreams; You've given me everything I've ever needed, everything a person could want in this life. Please, let me give it back to You." I raised my hands in front of me, open and cupped; this was the answer to the vision of Jesus that I had. I was very humbled by this, and I could feel the presence of the Spirit while I was praying.

After saying this prayer, I felt more of the Spirit enter through the top of my head. Again, I felt some minor (painless) movement inside my head. What this movement was, in my understanding, was God helping me to tap into parts of my brain which most human beings never tap into. I can remember teachers in school referring to people as being left-brained or right-brained. I am grateful to now be "fully-brained"—thank You, God. As I mentioned, this was not something I premeditated, but looking back it was one of the best, most positive things I have ever done. I read about this type of prayer only days later in Romans 12:1-2: "I beseech you therefore, brethren, by the mercies of God, that you present your bodies a living sacrifice, holy, acceptable to God, which is your reasonable service. And do not be conformed to this world, but be transformed by the renewing of your mind, that you may prove what is that good and acceptable and perfect will of God."

I now understand what Jesus was talking about in the following Scripture: "Render therefore to Caesar the things that are Caesar's, and to God the things that are God's" (Matthew 22:21). The following

Scripture from the apostle Paul began to make sense to me as well: "Do you not know that your body is the temple of the Holy Spirit who is in you, whom you have from God, and you are not your own? For you were bought at a price; therefore glorify God in your body and in your spirit, which are God's" (1 Corinthians 6:19-20). I now understand that my body is on loan from my Creator, and I shall do my best to take care of the one body I will ever have. I also found that giving it back to God keeps me safe, happy, sane, joyful, helpful, patient, nonjudgmental, and spiritually awake. God helps me to be the person He created me to be, which is in His image. I thoroughly appreciate the true gifts He has given me in this life; and the more I continue to walk away from the path of destruction, the more He trusts me and the more He heals me from the inside out. God takes care of me mentally, physically, and spiritually, and I am grateful to have Him in my life.

As I continued on my journey of faith, I began to gain a better understanding of Jesus of Nazareth (the Christ). In the beginning of my journey, I'll admit I wasn't sure about Jesus. It took me about a month of spiritual growth to accept Him as my Savior. I suppose the reason for this is that I needed to find the Father (the Spirit of God) before I would be able to understand His teachings. He said it Himself in the following Scriptures:

"No one can come to Me unless the Father who sent Me draws him; and I will raise him up at the last day. It is written in the prophets, "And they shall all be taught by God." [Isaiah 54:13] Therefore everyone who has heard and learned from the Father comes to Me." (John 6:44-45)

I didn't have the spiritual know-how in the past to understand the depth of His teachings; however, in waking up spiritually, things began to make sense. I understand wholeheartedly that Jesus was God living as a man: "I and My Father are one" (John 10:30). "Do you not believe that I am in the Father, and the Father in Me? The words that I speak to you I do not speak on my own authority; but the Father who dwells in Me does the works. Believe Me that I am in the Father and the Father in Me, or else believe Me for the sake of the works themselves" (John 14:10-11).

In my understanding, Jesus knew that the Spirit of God was inside of Him: "But concerning the resurrection of the dead, have you not read what was spoken to you by God, saying, 'I am the God of Abraham, the God of Isaac, and the God of Jacob'? God is not the God of the dead, but of the living" (Matthew 22:31-32). "For He is not the God of the dead but of the living, for all live to Him" (Luke 20:38). "I am the resurrection and the life. He who believes in Me, though he may die, he shall live" (John 11:25).

Jesus is talking about the spiritual resurrection and the spiritual awakening. Experience showed me that my selfish, prideful, resentful, sinful self had to be put to rest (die) so that I could live spiritually awake. Jesus spoke the truth all the time; He loved everybody; He helped people everywhere He went; He healed people; and He even prophesized His own death:

> Now Jesus, going up to Jerusalem, took the twelve disciples aside on the road and said to them, "Behold, we are going up to Jerusalem, and the Son of Man will be betrayed to the chief priests and to the scribes; and they will condemn Him to death, and deliver Him to the Gentiles to mock and to scourge and to crucify. And the third day He will rise again." (Matthew 20:17-19)

Jesus knew all of this because He was getting His information from the Spirit of the Father. He predicted the destruction of the temple:

> Then Jesus went out and departed from the temple, and His disciples came up to show Him the buildings of the temple. And Jesus said to them, "Do you not see all these things? Assuredly I say to you, not one stone shall be left here upon another, that shall not be thrown down." (Matthew 24:1-2)

All of this happened, just as He said it would, after He died on the cross:

> And Jesus cried out again with a loud voice, and yielded up His spirit. Then, behold, the veil of the temple was torn in two from top to bottom; and the earth quaked, and the rocks were split, and the graves were opened; and many bodies of the saints who had fallen asleep were raised; and coming out of the graves after His resurrection, they went into the holy city and appeared to many. (Matthew 27:50-53)

I must also note that Jerusalem and the Temple were destroyed in AD 70 by the Roman army under the emperor Titus, which fulfilled Jesus' prophesy of the Temple's destruction.

Now, as I understand this, the body of Jesus died because He chose to die. When He cried out, His Spirit was released from His body. The Jews did not accept Him as Messiah; the wise ones, however, understood that Jesus was speaking God's word and providing an example of how God would live in human form on His green earth; away from sin, and full of love and compassion for mankind. In living without sin, Jesus was completely trusted by God, and He was able to heal people and perform miracles: Matthew 14:13—Jesus feeding the five thousand; Matthew 20:29—two blind men receive their sight; John 11:38—Jesus raises Lazarus from the dead.

Many people saw Him perform these miracles; who am I to say that He did not? I understand the healing powers of the Holy Spirit from my own experiences because I have personally *felt* the healing powers of the Spirit, but I was unable to feel them until I began walking away from the negative ways of my past. Jesus lived His life one precious moment at a time, one simple day at a time, because He knew His time here on earth would not be of great length. Jesus mourned for Jerusalem:

> "O Jerusalem, Jerusalem, the one who kills the prophets and stones those who are sent to her! How often I wanted to gather

your children together, as a hen gathers her chicks under her wings, but you were not willing! See! Your house is left to you desolate; for I say to you, you shall see Me no more till you say, 'Blessed is He who comes in the name of the LORD!'"(Matthew 23:37-39)

It was not Jesus speaking, but the Spirit of God speaking through Jesus, because God had tried for so long to bring His people together in the Holy Land, but the people just did not have the ears to hear, and they had strayed from His commandments. Jesus did not want to die, however, He knew that it was God's will for Him to die so that sins may be forgiven:

He went a little farther and fell on His face, and prayed, saying, "O My Father, if it is possible, let this cup pass from Me; nevertheless, not as I will, but as You will." (Matthew 26:39) Again, a second time, He went away and prayed, saying, "O My Father, if this cup cannot pass away from Me unless I drink it, Your will be done." (Matthew 26:42)

And He said, "Abba, Father, all things are possible for You. Take this cup away from Me; nevertheless, not what I will, but what You will." (Mark 14:36)

"Father, if it is Your will, take this cup away from Me; nevertheless not My will, but Yours, be done." (Luke 22:42)

Jesus spoke these words, lifted up His eyes to heaven, and said: "Father, the hour has come. Glorify Your Son, that Your Son also may glorify You, as You have given Him authority over all flesh, that He should give eternal life to as many as You have given Him. And this is eternal life, that they may know You, the only true God, and Jesus Christ whom You have sent. I have glorified You on the earth. I have finished the work which You have given Me to do. And now, O Father, glorify Me together with Yourself, with the glory which I had with You before the world was." (John 17:1-5)

Again, Jesus had an immense purpose in His life: to provide an example of godly living, to teach the truth about God, to show love for everyone, and to bear the burden of sin for all of us:

Surely He has borne our griefs and carried our sorrows; yet we esteemed Him stricken, smitten by God, and afflicted. But He was wounded for our transgressions, He was bruised for our iniquities; the chastisement for our peace was upon Him, and by His stripes we are healed. All we like sheep have gone astray; we have turned, every one, to his own way; and the LORD has laid on Him the iniquity of us all. (Isaiah 53:4-6)

Had Jesus not done what He had done, I would not be alive today. I thank Him humbly every day for what He did for all of us, and the example of living He provided. Never again shall I take His name in vain.

PROPHETS

In gaining a better understanding of the life and teachings of Jesus, I understand why He is seated at the right hand of the Father. Jesus was and still is God's right-hand man; the body of Jesus died, but the name and the Spirit of Jesus will never die because of the billions of human beings who have lived happy, healthy, meaningful, sober, spiritual lives by following His teachings. People who have been born of the Spirit (a spiritual awakening) will understand that Jesus was God in the flesh. Jesus is still saving souls today, He's certainly saved mine.

I have also gained a more thorough understanding of God's true prophets. True prophets, such as Moses, Ezekiel, Elijah, Jeremiah, Daniel, and Isaiah were people who knew God intimately, and they do not promote hatred towards anyone. These prophets had visions and dreams, and were touched by the Spirit of God. True prophets teach the truth and help people to live better lives. Moses, for example, was chosen by God to deliver His people out of slavery in Egypt. In Exodus 3, Moses went up to Mount Sinai (also known as Mount Horeb) a man and came back down completely saturated with the Spirit of God:

> Then Moses said to the LORD, "O my Lord, I am not eloquent, neither before nor since You have spoken to Your servant; but I am slow of speech and slow of tongue." So the LORD said to him, "Who has made man's mouth? Or who makes the mute, the deaf, the seeing, or the blind? Have not I, the LORD? Now therefore, go, and I will be with your mouth and teach you what you shall say." But he said, "O my Lord, please send by the hand of whomever else You may send."

> So the anger of the LORD was kindled against Moses, and He said: "Is not Aaron the Levite your brother? I know that he can speak well. And look, he is also coming out to meet you. When he sees you, he will be glad in his heart. Now you shall speak to him and put the words in his mouth. And I will be with your mouth and with his mouth, and I will teach you what you shall do. So he shall be your spokesman to the people. And he himself shall be as a mouth for you, and you shall be to him as God. And you shall take this rod in your hand, with which you shall do the signs." (Exodus 4:10-17)

Moses was the voice of God; Moses is the human being to whom God revealed His Ten Commandments, and Moses wrote the books of Genesis, Exodus, Leviticus, Numbers, and Deuteronomy (the five books which compose the Hebrew Torah). He wrote Genesis and Exodus after the events happened, because He was getting his information from the Spirit.

Another great prophet, or man of God, was Elijah:

Now it happened after these things that the son of the woman who owned the house became sick. And his sickness was so serious that there was no breath left in him. So she said to Elijah, "What have I to do with you, O man of God? Have you come to me to bring my sin to remembrance, and to kill my son?" And he said to her, "Give me your son." So he took him out of her arms and carried him to the upper room where he was staying, and laid him on his own bed. Then he cried out to the LORD and said, "O LORD my God, have You also brought tragedy on the widow with whom I lodge, by killing her son?" And he stretched himself out on the child three times, and cried out to the LORD and said, "O LORD my God, I pray, let this child's soul come back to him." Then the LORD heard the voice of Elijah; and the soul of the child came back to him, and he revived.

And Elijah took the child and brought him down from the upper room into the house, and gave him to his mother. And Elijah said, "See, your son lives!" Then the woman said to Elijah, "Now by this I know that you are a man of God, and that the word of the LORD in your mouth is the truth." (1 Kings 17:17-24)

Lay-people do not understand the teachings of these prophets because most people wait for a miracle to come to them rather than seeking the Father sincerely, honestly, and humbly; thus most people have never felt the presence of the Spirit:

"Blessed are you when they revile and persecute you, and say all kinds of evil against you falsely for My sake. Rejoice and be exceedingly glad, for great is your reward in heaven, for so they persecuted the prophets who were before you." (Matthew 5:11-12)

"But blessed are your eyes for they see, and your ears for they hear; for assuredly, I say to you that many prophets and righteous men desired to see what you see, and did not see it, and to hear what you hear, and did not hear it." (Matthew 13:16-17)

"For many are called, but few are chosen." (Matthew 22:14)

GOD (THE HOLY SPIRIT)

God, as I understand Him, represents all that is good and positive. He is an invisible God (a spirit): "No one has seen God at any time. If we love one another, God abides in us, and His love has been perfected in us. By this we know that we abide in Him, and He in us, because He has given us of His Spirit" (1 John 4:12-13). He is a God of emotions, real human emotions and positive character traits; love, peace, honesty, forgiveness, humility, helpfulness, kindness, joy, open-mindedness, truth, willingness (to help people)—all of the emotions, dear reader, which we all had as newborn children. In regards to love, a person cannot *see* love; a person can *feel* love and see acts of love. I know I love a person if I feel it in my heart; I *believe* it, I *feel* it, I *know* it, and then I show it. Just like God, I can *feel* the presence of God, and I can *see* acts of God. I *believe* in God, I *feel* His presence, and I *know* He is real. The following Scripture is probably the best definition for love that I have ever come across:

"Love suffers long and is kind; love does not envy; love does not parade itself, is not puffed up; does not behave rudely, does not seek its own, is not provoked, thinks no evil; does not rejoice in iniquity, but rejoices in truth; bears all things, believes all things, hopes all things, endures all things. Love never fails. But whether there are prophecies, they will fail; whether there are tongues, they will cease; whether there is knowledge, it will vanish away. For we know in part and we prophesy in part. But when that which is perfect has come, then that which is in part will be done away.

When I was a child, I spoke as a child, I understood as a child, I thought as a child; but when I became a man, I put away childish things. For now we see in a mirror, dimly, but then face to face. Now I know in part, but then I shall know just as I also am known. And now abide faith, hope, love, these three; but the greatest of these is love." (1 Corinthians 13:4-13)

Which brings me again to the teachings of Jesus: "God is Spirit, and those who worship Him must worship in spirit and truth" (John 4:24). "If the world hates you, you know that it hated Me before it hated you" (John 15:18). In my understanding, Jesus is talking about Himself, but He is also talking about the life of a human being. In my experience, as a child I did not know how to hate until someone hated me; I did not know how to feel pain until someone hurt me; I did not know how to lie until someone lied to me; I did not know how to steal until I witnessed somebody else do it. All of the negative emotions that I was not born to feel were caused by negative outside influences. They were learned behaviors. God did not create me to be hateful and negative; the world brought that on me. Through the grace of God, the Holy Spirit, and thorough self-inquiry and evaluation, I have given up the word *hate* because being hateful and negative is a waste of my precious time and it is not the works of God. I refer to God's Ultimate Truth as the GUT instinct. In my experience, when I go against my gut, it usually leads me into trouble. Through following the twelve steps and praying sincerely and thoroughly, God has given me back all of my emotions as well as my conscience, and I feel like a brand-new person.

THE UNHOLY SPIRIT (SATAN)

The name Satan comes from *Ha-Satan*, which in Hebrew means "the adversary." The devil represents all that is unholy. That includes all those negative emotions and negative character traits that as human beings we are *not* meant to feel or possess—excessive pride, greed, lust, anger, gluttony, envy/jealousy, sloth, hatred, lies, selfishness, doubt, blame, resentment. Satan wants us to think that *seeing* is *believing*, but it is actually the opposite: *believing* is *seeing*, as I mentioned in the previous section. When a person waits to see something happen, it is far too late to do anything about it; and if a person lives his or her life under this false notion, he/she is in for many disappointments. Satan is tricky; he works against us almost as soon as we come out of the womb:

> "And you He [God] made alive, who were dead in trespasses and sins, in which you once walked according to the course of this world, according to the prince of the power of the air, the spirit [Satan] who now works in the sons of disobedience, among whom also we all once conducted ourselves in the lusts of our flesh, fulfilling the desires of the flesh and of the mind, and were by nature children of wrath, just as the others." (Ephesians 2:1-3)

> Jesus answered, "It is he to whom I shall give a piece of bread when I have dipped it." And having dipped the bread, He gave it to Judas Iscariot, the son of Simon. Now after the piece of bread, Satan entered him. Then Jesus said to him, "What you do, do quickly." (John 13:26-27)

> Then Satan entered Judas, surnamed Iscariot, who was numbered among the twelve. (Luke 22:3)

Now, in my understanding, Satan entered Judas in the form of anger, jealousy, envy, and selfishness because Jesus had something that nobody could see (a Soul inside of Him—the Holy Spirit), and Judas wanted what He had. But he didn't understand it, so he was jealous and envious, and decided to betray Him for money (something he could see—a possession).

Here are some examples of how this slimy little serpent (Satan) has worked against me in my life: the teacher who said, "You can't be president." Well, that teacher lied to me. I could have been president; a human being has done it before and it is proven that it can be done. It would have taken some faith and some hard work, but it was absolutely possible. However, since this unsuspecting teacher decided to speak without thinking, he or she unwittingly deprived a child of his/her life ambitions. The teacher had become an unsuspecting vessel for the unholy spirit. You should stay away from any negative person who tells you, dear reader, what you cannot do or what you cannot be; they are not going to help you in your life.

Another example that comes to mind was during one of the first twelve-step meetings I attended after the two-week program. An angry man said, "This will be the hardest thing you will ever do in your life." That man knew nothing about me whatsoever, and he lied to me. He was trying to get me to turn back and keep me out of the light; just another example of the unholy spirit working through an unsuspecting person. I'll admit, my journey has not been easy, but nothing in life that is worthwhile ever is. Although I must say, growing in faith and a willingness to make positive life changes became easier and easier with each passing day, by the grace of God. About thirty days into my journey, I stopped counting the days, because I realized that life is really about living for the day and making each day count. Why wouldn't a person want to feel good every day? I still cannot find an answer to that question. There came a point where I was able to live in the moment; I stopped worrying about the future and really started living. It seems to me that the speed of life is one moment at a time, one day at a time. As Jesus said:

"Therefore do not worry about tomorrow, for tomorrow will worry about its own things. Sufficient for the day is its own trouble." (Matthew 6:34)

Jesus said to them, "If God were your Father, you would love Me, for I proceeded forth and came from God; nor have I come of

Myself, but He sent Me. Why do you not understand My speech? Because you are not able to listen to My word. You are of your father the devil, and the desires of your father you want to do. He was a murderer from the beginning, and does not stand in the truth, because there is no truth in him. When he speaks a lie, he speaks from his own resources, for he is a liar and the father of it. But because I tell the truth, you do not believe Me. Which of you convicts Me of sin? And if I tell the truth, why do you not believe Me? He who is of God hears God's words; therefore you do not hear, because you are not of God." (John 8:42-47)

Another example of the serpent trying to destroy my dreams would be the example I provided in chapter 4 regarding the athletic director and baseball coach who tried to get me to lie and deter me from the right path. In my understanding, Adolf Hitler is a perfect example of a human being completely saturated with the unholy spirit (Satan). Do you think it is a coincidence that Hitler wanted to exterminate the Jews? Satan hates God, so what the slimy serpent does is he tries to get back at God by killing people, namely God's chosen people, the Jews.

Personally, there came a point when I realized that Satan isn't just going to walk up to me and say, "Hey Mike I have a plan for your life. I'll start by helping you get hooked on smoking cigarettes at a young age. Next, hey let's have a drink, maybe try some drugs; it will make you feel great. I will stay with you your whole life, and I will help you make the wrong decision in any given situation. Go ahead, cheat on your spouse, she'll never find out. Neglect your children, I'll help you waste every precious moment. I will help you convince yourself that you're worthy of nothing, and that life is meaningless. I will help you convince yourself that you're always right and it is okay to be hateful, prejudiced, and racist. I will be your conscience. I will do all this with you, and the whole truth is it will not be you who is living your life, but it will be my filthy spirit living your life for you—and you will have no clue that this is even happening. I will help you make God the scapegoat for all of the problems in your life; or better yet, I will help you believe He doesn't exist. I will keep you spiritually dead so you can spread my filth and negativity wherever you go. I am powerful, crafty, and cunning; I have stolen the lives of billions and I am pleased. The only way to defeat me is with the power of God, but I will keep you confused and spiritually dead so I can keep you from seeking Him. I will help you destroy yourself slowly but surely. I am a parasite; you cannot see me, but I am here to destroy. When you only exist, I live; and when you live, I only exist." True, the devil is not going to approach me and tell me these things, but what he will do is work through people who are under his cloud of spiritual deadness to guide me down the wrong path in life and keep me away from God. I have found that Satan is afraid of God, and as I continued to seek God, the devil got out of my life in a hurry. "Therefore submit to God. Resist the devil and he will flee from you. Draw near to God and He will draw near to you" (James 4:7).

THE HOLY TRINITY

The *Father* speaks to an awakened soul through the conscience (His voice in the human head). The Son, Jesus, is the beating heart; full of living waters, love, honesty, kindness, integrity, perseverance, willingness, and truth (*positive emotions*). The *Holy Spirit* is left upon the shoulders of the individual to find by first becoming honest with one's self, and thoroughly examining one's own life through self-examination in order to learn to be honest with others. I realize that I cannot expect to be honest with anyone if I do not first learn to be honest with myself. I now understand that to lie to myself is to lie to the One who created me (God). I followed the simple steps just as they are written and cleaned my own house with a thorough moral inventory before I could try to help anyone else. It reminds me of the following: "Woe to you, scribes and Pharisees, hypocrites! For you cleanse the outside of the cup and dish, but inside they are full of extortion and self-indulgence. Blind Pharisee, first cleanse the inside of the cup and dish, that the outside of them may be clean also" (Matthew 23:25-26). With God's help, I needed to thoroughly examine my life to work on myself and my flaws, sins, self-destructive behavior, and defects of character, before I could teach others. If I had not helped myself first, and had a spiritual awakening, I would have been trying to share something that I did not have. In truth, I put my heart and soul into the twelve steps, and that is just what I got out of it; a new Heart and a Soul. I must note that I am not saying that "God tells me to do things." That is not how it works. What God does do is give guidance, wisdom, and insight to help the individual make the best decision in any given life circumstance.

THE PERSISTENCE OF EVIL

The question has been asked, *If God is loving and forgiving, and He represents all that is good and just, then why is evil so evident in our world today, and why has it been so persistent throughout history?* The Master explains this better than I can in The Parable of the Wheat and the Tares:

Another parable He put forth to them, saying: "The kingdom of heaven is like a man who sowed good seed in his field; but while men slept, his enemy came and sowed tares among the wheat and went his way. But when the grain had sprouted and produced a crop, then the tares also appeared. So the servants of the owner came and said to him, 'Sir, did you not sow good seed in your field? How then does it have tares?' He said to them, 'An enemy has done this.' The servants said to him, 'Do you want us then to go and gather them up?' But he said, 'No, lest while you gather up the tares you also uproot the wheat with them. Let both grow together until the harvest, and at the time of harvest I will say to the reapers, "First gather together the tares and bind them in bundles to burn them, but gather the wheat into my barn.""" (Matthew 13:24-30)

The Parable of the Wheat and the Tares explained:

Jesus said to His disciples, "He who sows the good seed is the Son of Man. The field is the world, the good seeds are the sons of the kingdom, but the tares are the sons of the wicked one. The enemy who sowed them is the devil, the harvest is the end of the age, and the reapers are the angels. Therefore as the tares are gathered and burned in the fire, so it will be at the end of this age. The Son of Man will send out His angels, and they will gather out of His kingdom all things that offend, and those who practice lawlessness, and will cast them into the furnace of fire. There will be wailing and gnashing of teeth. Then the righteous will shine forth as the sun in the kingdom of their Father. He who has ears to hear, let him hear!" (Matthew 13:37-43)

KNOWLEDGE AND WISDOM

As I continued to grow with God and seek Him through prayer and self-evaluation, He continued to guide me spiritually and He granted me knowledge and wisdom. Here are some of the spiritual teachings of the Master:

Jesus answered and said to them, "Destroy this temple, and in three days I will raise it up." (John 2:19)

Michael's insight: It is obvious that the temple He was talking about was His body which was resurrected on the third day (as noted in John 2:21-22).

Jesus answered and said to him, "Most assuredly, I say to you, unless one is born again, he cannot see the kingdom of God." (John 3:3)

Michael's insight: Having been born of the Spirit, I am able to really see and appreciate the beauty of this world: The planet Earth which the almighty invisible Spirit of the universe rotates for all of us to give us beautiful sunrises in the direction of the east and beautiful sunsets in the direction of the west. I am now able to see the beauty of the sun that lights the day, and the moon and stars which He shines for us all, to give us light during the dark hours of the night. The mountains, the rivers, the oceans, the plants, the animals—everything is His. The kingdom of God is within me, just as He said. In my past I didn't have the eyes to see how beautiful life really is. I also understand that I will not enter heaven unless I have a spiritual awakening/a soul.

> Jesus answered, "Most assuredly, I say to you, unless one is born of water and the Spirit, he cannot enter the kingdom of God." (John 3:5)

Michael's insight: To be born of water means to be baptized. To be born of the Spirit means to have a spiritual awakening and to receive Life. The Spirit has made me fully alive, mind, body, and soul.

> "That which is born of the flesh is flesh, and that which is born of the Spirit is spirit. Do not marvel that I said to you, 'You must be born again.'" (John 3:6-7)

Michael's insight: I began to understand that prayer and self-evaluation provided by the twelve steps was helping me to be reborn. Simply put, my spirit/soul, which had been dead, was now waking up, and I was unlearning many of the lies I had been brainwashed with on my walk through life. I was receiving back a clear conscience, which until then had been warped by my poor habits and the sinful nature of this world. It is not about defining myself as "a born again," it is about being reborn and receiving the memories of my life, as well as all of my God-given emotions. These spiritual teachings offered immense insight at this point in my journey because no human wisdom could understand or help me understand what was really happening in my life; it required God's wisdom.

"The wind blows where it wishes, and you hear the sound of it, but cannot tell where it comes from and where it goes. So is everyone who is born of the Spirit." (John 3:8)

Michael's insight: Having been born of the Spirit, I began to recognize that the majority of people walking this Earth are spiritually dead and have little to no awareness of life or who they really are. Very few fully understand the joy, love, truth, and simplicity of being in the Spirit.

"No one has ascended to heaven but He who came down from heaven, that is, the Son of Man who is in heaven." (John 3:13)

Michael's insight: Jesus is talking about the Spirit of God inside of His body, which had come from heaven. He is saying that unless what is inside of me (Spirit) has been given to me from above, I will not enter. Unless I am of God, I shall not enter God's kingdom.

"And as Moses lifted up the serpent in the wilderness, even so must the Son of Man be lifted up, that whoever believes in Him should not perish but have eternal life.

For God so loved the world that He gave His only begotten Son, that whoever believes in Him should not perish but have everlasting life. For God did not send His Son into the world to condemn the world, but that the world through Him might be saved.

He who believes in Him is not condemned; but he who does not believe is condemned already, because he has not believed in the name of the only begotten Son of God.

And this is the condemnation, that the light has come into the world, and men loved darkness rather than light, because their deeds were evil.

For everyone practicing evil hates the light and does not come to the light, lest his deeds should be exposed. But he who does the truth comes to the light, that his deeds may be clearly seen, that they have been done in God." (John 3:14-21)

Michael's insight: In being born of the Spirit, I began to understand the power behind Jesus's spiritual truths. I also began to notice how many people would rather practice evil and live a lie; so many people seem to prefer a life of sin and hatred; worshipping money, job titles, and socioeconomic status. I refer to it as the "Great Façade." It made me sad to see so few genuine people around me, but I accepted it because I was the same way prior to having a spiritual awakening. I also began to understand that just by being honest about myself and speaking openly about my past, I was now coming into the light. The negative ways of my past were being forgiven (my deeds were being exposed), and I was becoming one of His chosen people. I also began to understand the truth. I understand that when a person speaks of his/her own life experiences, that person is telling the truth, and truth is the Word of God. When I speak, I speak of my life experiences. If someone asks me something I have never experienced in my life, I simply say, "I don't know." Otherwise I am unwittingly lying and possibly sending that person down the wrong path. "But let your 'Yes' be 'Yes,' and your 'No,' 'No.' For whatever is more than these is from the evil one" (Matthew 5:37).

Jesus said to them, "Most assuredly, I say to you, before Abraham was, I AM." (John 8:58)

Michael's insight: In my understanding, Jesus is talking about the Spirit inside of Him; the Spirit of God which had been around since the beginning.

Jesus said to him, "I am the way, the truth, and the life. No one comes to the Father except through Me." (John 14:6)

Michael's insight: In striving to live the way Jesus lived (love, truth, and simplicity; one day at a time; one precious moment at a time), I have come to understand that His way is Life.

Pilate therefore said to Him, "Are You a king then?" Jesus answered, "You say rightly that I am a king. For this cause I was born, and for this cause I have come into the world, that I should bear witness to the truth. Everyone who is of the truth hears My voice." (John 18:37)

Michael's insight: In my understanding, God came down from heaven in the form of a man named Jesus to give testimony and teach the truth about God. He is the King of kings. In growing spiritually, I began to hear the Spirit when a person would speak the truth based on his or her life experiences. I began to understand that truth is the Word of God working/speaking through a person.

Here are some quotes that have given me insight and helped me along my journey:

"Love doesn't make the world go around. Love is what makes the ride worthwhile."—Franklin Jones

"When angry, count to ten. When very angry, a hundred."—Thomas Jefferson

"I shall pass through this world but once. If, therefore, there be any kindness I can show, or any good thing I can do, let me do it now; let me not defer it or neglect it, for I shall not pass this way again."—Étienne de Grellet

"Humility is not thinking less of yourself but thinking of yourself less."—C.S. Lewis

"It is human nature to think wisely and act foolishly."—Anatole France

"The supreme truth to which the Torah gives witness is that one who is not in my image—whose creed, culture or color is not like mine—is nonetheless in God's image. That is the principle of the dignity of difference."—Rabbi Jonathan Sacks

"There is a principle which is a bar against all information, which is proof against all arguments and which cannot fail to keep a man in everlasting ignorance—that principle is contempt prior to investigation."—Herbert Spencer

"Death is not the greatest loss in life. The greatest loss is what dies inside us while we live."—Norman Cousins

"Let us help people to reach their full potential, catch them doing something *right*."—R. Bruce Blomberg

"The ablest men in all walks of life are men of faith."—Bruce Barton

"When a man has pity on all living creatures, then only is he noble."—Buddha

"The unexamined life is not worth living"—Socrates

CHAPTER FIVE

The End

Two thousand years ago, a governor by the name of Pontius Pilate asked a question. "Pilate said to Him [Jesus], 'What is truth?'"(John 18:38). Well, Governor Pilate, to answer your question, I recognize and understand the truth. I understand that when a person speaks of his/her life experiences, that person is speaking the truth. Truth is the works of a godly person. I understand that I only know something to be true if I have lived it and experienced it in my life. If and when somebody asks me a question about something I have never experienced, the correct answer is, "I don't know." It is not about being "holier than thou"; it is about being an honest human being.

In thoroughly following the twelve steps, many miracles happened in my life. I met more honest, truthful people, and found true humility. It brings me joy to know that there is still some good in this world. Another miracle is that I found the Spirit of God. As I continued to grow in faith, prayer, and self-inquiry, eventually God gave me back my conscience (which is His voice, in my head). I understand, based on my life experiences and my step work, that God knows *everything* about me. He knew every sin I had committed because He watched me do it. He knew every lie I had ever told because He heard me speak it. I understand that the person I had really been lying to was me, and in lying to myself I was really lying to the One who made me.

The healing process began with a willingness to live a life of truth and honesty. I understand wholeheartedly that the spiritual change had to come from within. "Now when He was asked by the Pharisees when the kingdom of God would come, He answered them and said, 'The kingdom of God does not come with observation; nor will they say, "See here!" or "See there!" For indeed, the kingdom of God is within you'" (Luke 17:20-21). I also understand that the help had to come from above, as well as the positive, experienced, truthful people around me. The truth is, God did not make it difficult for me to find Him; it was other people, their jealousy, cynicism, and religious rules that were making it difficult. All I had to do was seek Him sincerely and honestly through prayer and self-inquiry. As I mentioned, God knows everything about me; He knows me better than any human being, and better than I know myself. He is the only One who has never lied to me; He is the only One who has always been there for me.

Every time I got into trouble, it was because I had gone against my conscience (that little voice of reason in my head) and I was punished for it. For example, a few years ago I was running on very little sleep, but still decided to meet some friends for beverages. The voice of reason said, *Mike go home and go to bed*, but another negative voice said, *Ah screw it, I said I would go*. Well, I now understand that this other little voice was not my conscience, it was the adversary, or the antithesis of my conscience; I'll leave it at that. I now understand that in going against my conscience, I was going against God, and I'm grateful that I have realized that, and I will not do that again. I also understand that throughout my life, God has been judging me righteously, based on my actions. For example, as I mentioned in chapter 4, when I was a young kid (elementary and middle school) I was quite overweight. It took some work to get in shape and be healthy. In high-school, I was in shape, but on one or two occasions I made the mistake of picking on another boy for being overweight, and

I was punished for it. The message was very simple: "Michael, do not forget where you have come from." After realizing that, I then would use my position of power as an athlete to stand up for people when they were being bullied. I realize that now, and I find it very important not to judge anyone, and to treat people with kindness, regardless of how they treat me.

In short, God has loved me since the day I was born, and in my experience, He loves me the way a Father would love a child: *unconditionally*. He knows I've made mistakes in my life, and all He asked was that I seek forgiveness of those mistakes and pursue an honest lifestyle. God does not give up on people; people give up on themselves and other people. God does not condemn people, it is our actions that condemn ourselves and our souls. I also now understand that in making amends to the people whom I had harmed, I was really seeking God's forgiveness, because He created those people too: "For He is not the God of the dead but of the living, for all live to Him" (Luke 20:38). The ones whom I did not get to make amends to, I prayed for them and asked God for forgiveness.

As I continued to grow along my journey, the following Scriptures began to make sense to me:

"In the beginning was the Word, and the Word was with God, and the Word was God" (John 1:1). In my understanding, this is in reference to the beginning of time, Creation, when the Spirit of God spoke everything into existence (Genesis 1). What it also means is the beginning of the life of a human being. When a child is born, that child has both a soul and a conscience; plain and simple. God is living inside the body of that child:

Therefore let that abide in you which you heard from the beginning. If what you heard from the beginning abides in you, you also will abide in the Son and in the Father. And this is the promise that He has promised us—eternal life. (1 John 2:24-25)

You are of God, little children, and have overcome them, because He who is in you is greater than he who is in the world. (1 John 4:4)

Have you ever noticed how children seem to say such profound things? "At that time Jesus answered and said, 'I thank You, Father, Lord of heaven and earth, that You have hidden these things from the wise and prudent and have revealed them to babes. Even so, Father, for so it seemed good in Your sight'" (Matthew 11:25-26). Children are happy, children have hopes and dreams; children are really *alive*. Do you remember, dear reader, how as children, life was much more joyful and happy? Well, I tell you the truth, you can feel like that again, without false chemical highs. Jesus said, "Assuredly I say to you, unless you are converted and become as little children, you will by no means enter the kingdom of heaven. Therefore whoever humbles himself as this little child is the greatest in the kingdom of heaven. Whoever receives one little child like this in My name receives Me" (Matthew 18:3-5). It does not have to be difficult; I have done it, which proves that any human being can do it. I can remember a very negative person once said, "Children should be seen and not heard." That is a very evil, pessimistic thing to say, if you ask me. I would also like to share the following teachings of the apostle Paul:

However, we speak wisdom among those who are mature, yet not the wisdom of this age, nor of the rulers of this age, who are coming to nothing. But we speak the wisdom of God in a mystery, the hidden wisdom which God ordained before the ages for our glory, which none of the rulers of this age knew; for had they known, they would not have crucified the Lord of glory.

But as it is written: "Eye has not seen, nor ear heard, nor have entered into the heart of man the things which God has prepared for those who love Him." But God has revealed them to us through His Spirit. For the Spirit searches all things, yes, the deep things of God. For what man knows the things of a man except the spirit of the man which is in him? Even so no one knows the things of God except the Spirit of God." (1 Corinthians 2:6-11)

How God Works

The Spirit of God works through people; through Him, with Him, and in Him; in the unity of the Holy Spirit. This is a doxology which is said during the Eucharist by a priest. (A doxology is a hymn or verse in Christian liturgy glorifying God. Eucharist is a Christian sacrament commemorating the Last Supper by consecrating bread and wine. Consecration is a solemn commitment of your life or your time to some cherished purpose [to a service or goal].) In my understanding, this is really talking about people, not just Jesus. If it were only referring to Jesus, that would mean that my life, and your life mean absolutely nothing. This is referring to human beings, when a human being has a spiritual awakening and begins living under grace. God works through good people; He places positive thoughts into people's heads so we can help other people. He works through people to help people. He works through some of us more than others, unfortunately.

For example, God worked through Noah to build the ark (Genesis 6:13-22). God worked through people to create the enlightenment era. God worked through people to create the renaissance era. He worked through Christopher Columbus to prove that the world is round, and He wanted Christopher to prove it regardless of what the royalty told him, because that was Christopher Columbus's life purpose. God worked through George Washington to lead in the American Revolution. Many people looked to George Washington for answers, and he was getting his guidance from the Holy Spirit, as God spoke to him through his conscience. Another example, one of my personal heroes, is a man named Bill Wilson, the cofounder of the original twelve-step program. Here is what happened to Bill while he was in the hospital:

"There I humbly offered myself to God, as I then understood Him, to do with me as He would. I placed myself unreservedly under His care and direction. I admitted for the first time that of myself I was nothing; that without Him I was lost. I ruthlessly faced my sins and became willing to have my newfound Friend take them away root and branch. I have not had a drink since. My schoolmate visited me, and I fully acquainted him with my problems and deficiencies. We made a list of people I had hurt or toward whom I felt resentment. I expressed my entire willingness to approach these individuals, admitting my wrong. Never was I to be critical of them. I was to right all such matters to the utmost of my ability. I was to test my thinking by the new God-consciousness within. Common sense would thus become un-common sense. I was to sit quietly when in doubt, asking only for direction and strength to meet problems as He would have me. Never was I to pray for myself, except as my requests bore on my usefulness to others. Then only might I expect to receive. But that would be in great measure.

My friend promised when these things were done I would enter upon a new relationship with my Creator; that I would have the elements of a way of living which answered all my problems. Belief in the power of God, plus enough willingness, honesty and humility to establish and maintain the new order of things, were the essential requirements.

Simple, but not easy; a price had to be paid. It meant destruction of self-centeredness. I must turn in all things to the Father of Light who presides over us all.

These were revolutionary and drastic proposals, but the moment I fully accepted them, the effect was electric. There was a sense of victory, followed by such a peace and serenity I had never known. There was utter confidence. I felt lifted up, as though the great clean wind of a mountaintop blew through and through. God comes to most men gradually, but His impact on me was sudden and profound."[1]

In my understanding, once Bill had done this and realized how simple it is to be saved, he was on a mission to help as many as he could. He must have realized, with time, that he could only save the willing. So perhaps the easiest thing to do was to share his experiences with others, put it all in a book, and outline it into twelve steps that anyone could follow. A twelve-step program is so simple it is borderline fool-proof; however, it is not people proof. The truth is, God worked through, with, and in the body of Bill Wilson to form the original twelve-step program; a program which has branched out to many twelve-step programs (including mine) and saved both the lives and the souls of the people who have followed. Bill Wilson would never know how many people he helped, but God will know, because God knows everything.

The truth is, there is only one God, just as there is only one you, only one me, only one of anybody. The name and the spirit of a person will live on based on our actions and contributions to society and humanity. For example, Dr. Martin Luther King Jr. was a man who, clearly, was touched by God's grace. The body of Dr. King died, but his name and his spirit are still helping people today because of what he stood for and who he was. Another example is Mother Teresa. On September 10, 1946 Mother Teresa (then Sister Teresa) received what she described as a "call within a call" while on a train from Siliguri in the northern plains of West Bengal, to Darjeeling in the foothills of the Himalayas. Sister Teresa had been touched by an overwhelming experience of God's grace, light, and love. This experience transformed her life, and she took the grace of God into the slums of Calcutta. Mother Teresa had a thorough understanding of Jesus's words "I thirst" and God's thirst and love for His creations. Mother Teresa also understood the meaning of Matthew 25:40: "And the King will answer and say to them, 'Assuredly, I say to you, inasmuch as you did it to one of the least of these My brethren, you did it to Me.'" Mother Teresa was a living example of a human being who had been called by God, and she answered the call. She truly was a spiritual being clothed in a woman's body, and in my understanding is a more recent example of God's Spirit working through a living person. She helped more people than she'll ever know; but God will know, and her reward will be one of great highness, when the time comes.

Another example is Moses:

Then Moses said to God, "Indeed, when I come to the children of Israel and say to them, 'The God of your fathers has sent me to you,' and they say to me, 'What is His name?' what shall I say to them?" And God said to Moses, "I AM WHO I AM." And He said, "Thus you shall say to the children of Israel, 'I AM has sent me to you.'" Moreover God said to Moses, "Thus you shall say to the children of Israel: 'the LORD God of your fathers, the God of Abraham, the God of Isaac, and the God of Jacob, has sent me to you. This is My name forever, and this is My memorial to all generations.'" (Exodus 3:13-15)

I realize that this ancient scripture has perhaps been mistranslated over the centuries; the Hebrew of Exodus 3:14 is *Ehyeh asher ehyeh* which translates most nearly as "I will be what I will be." In this case, God is telling Moses that He cannot be predicted, controlled, or known in advance. In essence God is telling Moses to trust, have faith, and he will know when he sees what God will be, and not before. I can also relate this to my own experiences with God because I never know how He is going to intervene in my life until after the fact.

Moses went up to Mount Sinai as a man, and came back down completely saturated with the Spirit of God. "Thus says the LORD God of Israel: 'Let My people go, that they may hold a feast to Me in the wilderness'" (Exodus 5:1). "My people" is referring to God's people; the Hebrew people; the only ones who have been around since the beginning of time. Mark Twain once wrote:

"Jews constitute but one percent of the human race. It suggests a nebulous dim puff of star dust in the blaze of the Milky Way. Properly the Jew ought hardly to be heard of; but he is heard of. He is as prominent on this planet as any other people. His commercial importance is extravagantly out of proportion to the smallness of his bulk. His contributions to the world's list of great names in literature, science, art, music, medicine, and abstruse learning are also altogether out of proportion to the weakness of his numbers. He has made a marvelous fight in the world in all ages and he has done it with his hands tied behind him."[2]

The truth is Moses was the voice of God, the one whom God chose to deliver His people. If you, dear reader, wish to better understand this more thoroughly, it is all written in Exodus 7-12.

A couple more examples of God working through, with, and in a person would be Julia Child: God's will for her was to teach the world how to cook. The body of Julia Child died in 2004, but the name and spirit of Julia Child will never die, because she is still helping people today through her books, her recipes, and by the passionate example of how she lived, and what she has taught the world. Another example is Charles Darwin: "Okay Mr. Darwin, your life's ambition is to prove your theory, so I will work through you, with you, and in you to help you do so. Unfortunately, Mr. Darwin, you do not understand that there is no evolution without Spirit." God is working through me as I write this, and He is working through you, dear reader, as you read this. I'll refer again: "He is not the God of the dead, but the God of the living. You are therefore greatly mistaken" (Mark 12:27). Mohandas Gandhi is also a clear example of God's Spirit working through a person, and a life lived with purpose.

The most perfect and graceful example of God's Spirit working through, with, and living in a person is the Master, Jesus the Christ. God worked through Jesus to teach the truth, provide an example of how we should live, and bear the burden of sin for mankind:

"If you had known Me, you would have known My Father also; and from now on you know Him and have seen Him." Philip said to Him, "Lord, show us the Father, and it is sufficient for us." Jesus said to him, "Have I been with you so long, and yet you have not known Me, Philip? He who has seen Me has seen the Father; so how can you say, 'Show us the Father'? Do you not believe that I am in the Father, and the Father in Me? The words that I speak to you I do not speak on My own authority; but the Father who dwells in Me does the works. Believe Me that I am in the Father and the Father in Me, or else believe Me for the sake of the works themselves." (John 14:7-11)

The body of Jesus died and rose from the dead, but the name and the Spirit of Jesus will never die because of the billions of people who have lived healthy, happy, joyful, humble, sober, spiritual lives based on His teachings, and the truth that He is still saving souls two thousand years after His death. Jesus was God, living as a man.

I have noticed, in my journey through life that we live in a world full of people who love to tell everybody what they think. The truth is, I care very little about opinions and what people *think*; however, I absolutely do care and am interested in what people *know* based on their life experiences: their life, their journey, their truths, *realness*. It is a great tragedy that very few people in this world actually know how to listen to each other. I see it all the time with doctors, counselors, and even those who refer to themselves as "men and women of God." Always telling others what they think, yet having little to no understanding of the truth. It really is a shame. When someone starts a sentence with, "In my experience," a red flag goes off in my brain that says, *this person is telling the truth, time for me to listen, I just might learn a very valuable life lesson.* Some of the most valuable lessons in my life have cost me no money; all I had to pay was my attention. This is another reason why I love the twelve-step programs; it costs me no money to sit down and listen to a person open up and tell the truth based on his/her life experiences; it is a beautiful thing.

The truth is, God is everywhere; by grace and spiritual vision I am now able to see God's beauty in His creations, and I am able to see the beauty of how He creates through people: "For every house is built by someone, but He who built all things is God" (Hebrews 3:4). Jesus knew all of this, which is why He was not pleased when He entered the temple:

So they came to Jerusalem. Then Jesus went into the temple and began to drive out those who bought and sold in the temple, and overturned the tables of the money changers and the seats of those who sold doves. And He would not allow anyone to carry wares through the temple. Then He taught, saying to them, "Is it not written, *'My house shall be called a house of prayer for all nations'*? But you have made it a *'den of thieves.'"* [Jeremiah 7:11] (Mark 11:15-17).

Jesus knew that God had worked through King Solomon and his people to build the temple; (1 Kings 6:1-38). God controls everything, except Free Will. In my life experiences, it was my own free will that was sending me down the wrong path (the path of destruction, with one ending address: *hell*). I give my free will over to the Almighty every morning with a simple prayer: "Good morning, Abba. I thank You for this day, and for my life. Please help me to stay sober today, and please help me to use the voice You have given me to speak the truth in love. Please help me to remain patient and optimistic throughout the day. I put my life in Your hands, Your will, not mine, be done. Amen." This takes all of thirty seconds and in doing so, God keeps me happy, sane, joyful, and appreciative.

MOVIES

God teaches us through movies as well. An example of godly living is the movie *Forrest Gump.*[3] Forrest's mother told him not to let anyone tell him what he could not do or could not be. He realized that his legs didn't really need braces; some fat doctor who was miserable with his own life tried to force that belief on him. He listened to the good advice and ignored the bad advice. He made a deal with his friend Bubba to split everything 50/50, and he kept that promise even though Bubba died. The more money he made, the more he donated, and the more he helped people. He had everything he needed—love in his heart, peace in his mind, and joy in his soul. When he ran across country, he wasn't thinking about running and how much it hurt; he was too busy thinking about the woman he loved.

Forrest lived a very simple life, and he helped more people than he would ever know, just by being simple, positive, and honest. At one point in the movie he said to Lt. Dan, "Well, I'm going to heaven Lt. Dan," as if it was certain, and the truth is, yes, it was certain because he lived a simple life away from evil. Eventually his body would die, but his spirit would never die, because of all the people he helped. At another point in the movie, Forrest said something along the lines of, "I'm not a smart man, but I do know what love is." That is because he knew that love is an emotion; he couldn't see love, but he could feel it in his heart. He believed it, he felt it, and he knew it.

Frank Capra's *It's a Wonderful Life*[4] is another example of God teaching us through movies. In the beginning of this movie, all of the characters are praying for the story's lead character George Bailey. George is portrayed as an honest and helpful man. Early in the story, George's brother slipped through the ice while he and his friends were sledding. Without hesitation, George jumped right into the icy water to save his little brother. This act cost George the hearing in one of his ears, a pretty small price to pay in order to save the life of his little brother and watch him grow up to be an American war hero. Another example is when George saw the druggist putting poison into the capsules and wasn't sure what to do; he turned his head and saw a sign that said, "Ask dad, he knows," so he went to ask his father what he should do. When he reached his dad, he saw him doing the right thing, being honest, and leading by example, so George didn't even need to ask him. George knew that the druggist was not doing the right thing, so he corrected him, which in turn saved the lives of two people; the druggist, and the little boy who would have been poisoned by the capsules.

If you watch this movie closely, you'll notice how George never gave in to the earthly pleasures of money and wealth; he had ambitions, but he stayed behind to keep watch over his family and his hometown. Towards the end of the movie, he almost killed himself but he is saved by an answered prayer. The entire movie is about God's presence in the lives of human beings, and how God works through people to help other people through real friends. George had a spiritual awakening at the end of the movie because his guardian angel showed him what life would have been like if George Bailey had never been born; the whole town would have fallen into the hands of the devil (Mr. Potter; a greedy, hateful, sinful man) who wanted to rule and own everything, and everyone. Once George Bailey woke up spiritually, he realized he had everything a man could ever want: a beautiful wife, beautiful children, a nice house, and positive people (real friends) who cared about him. What the movie also showed is how the life of one person can have an immense impact on the lives of so many others. It makes me want to live the Golden Rule.

ANIMALS

God works through animals too. Animals are living creatures, and they can sense things (storms, weather patterns, etc.) that human beings cannot. It seems to me that animals can see what a person really looks like. For example, prior to my spiritual awakening, my fiancée's dog would growl at me and run away any time I would go with her to her parents' house. However, since I "woke up" and started living right, her dog is much friendlier to me, comes over to me, is happy to see me, and lets me pet him, etc. Another example of God working through animals is the following, from the book of Daniel:

"So the king gave the command, and they brought Daniel and cast him into the den of lions. But the king spoke, saying to Daniel, "Your God, whom you serve continually, He will deliver you." Then a stone was brought and laid on the mouth of the den, and the king sealed it with his own signet ring and the signets of his lords, that the purpose concerning Daniel might not be changed.

Now the king went to his palace and spent the night fasting; and no musicians were brought before him. Also his sleep went from him. Then the king arose very early in the morning and went in haste to the den of lions. And when he came to the den, he cried out with a lamenting voice to Daniel. The king spoke, saying to Daniel, "Daniel, servant of the living God, has your God, whom you serve continually, been able to deliver you from the lions?"

Then Daniel said to the king, "O king, live forever! My God sent His angel and shut the lions' mouths, so that they have not hurt me, because I was found innocent before Him; and also, O king, I have done no wrong before you." Now the king was exceedingly glad for him, and commanded that they should take Daniel up out of the den. So Daniel was taken up out of the den, and no injury whatever was found on him, because he believed in his God.

And the king gave the command, and they brought those men who had accused Daniel, and they cast them into the den of lions—them, their children, and their wives; and the lions overpowered them, and broke all their bones in pieces before they ever came to the bottom of the den." (Daniel 6:16-24)

The lions did not touch Daniel because they could see that he was pure and innocent, and Daniel had the Holy Spirit inside of him. The lions could therefore see how evil and deceitful the souls of his accusers were, and God did not save Daniel's accusers from being destroyed by the lions.

In closing about animals, I am grateful for how God has used animals, namely pets, to teach me to have love and compassion for other living creatures.

MUSIC AND SONGS

Here are some songs that move my soul:

"My Sweet Lord" by George Harrison
"Have I Told You Lately That I Love You" by Van Morrison
"Watching the Wheels" by John Lennon
"One Love" by Bob Marley
"Get Up Stand Up" by Bob Marley
"Redemption Song" by Bob Marley
"Thank You for Loving Me" by Jon Bon Jovi
"The Living Years" by Mike & the Mechanics
"Man in the Mirror" by Michael Jackson
"Oh Happy Day" by Edwin Hawkins
"Tears in Heaven" by Eric Clapton
"Tennessee" by Arrested Development
"One Day" by Matisyahu

If you, dear reader, listen to these songs and the lyrics, you may begin to understand where I am coming from. I can really relate to the lyrics in these songs, and having had a spiritual awakening I am now able to hear the true message. Listen to some of Bob Marley's lyrics from "One Love": "Let's get together to fight this holy Armageddon, so when the man come there will be no doom. Have pity on those whose chances grow thinner, there ain't no hiding place from the Father of Creation." And Michael Jackson's lyrics say, "You've got to stop it yourself brother." I realized that nobody can change me except me, and I am very grateful to have had the opportunity to slow down and take a look at my own life. I can relate to these songs directly, because I understand that these artists are sharing their message through music, as I am sharing my message through writing, and it is through God's grace that I am able to do so. I understand that God knows me better than anyone; there is no hiding from Him. Of course, there are many more beautiful songs, but I figured I would note these because it seems that any living person might be able to relate to the messages in each. I have mentioned having a relationship with God, and not a religion. The lyrics of Tennessee show me that I am not the only one who has found this, "Lord it's obvious we got a relationship, talking to each other every night and day. Although You're superior over me, we talk to each other in a friendship way."

Soul

The Spirit of God lives inside all of those who believe and have faith in Him. Some fortunate people lose neither their soul nor their conscience and live their entire lives in the light.

> "Therefore let that abide in you which you heard from the beginning. If what you heard from the beginning abides in you, you also will abide in the Son and in the Father. And this is the promise that He has promised us—eternal life. These things I have written to you concerning those who try to deceive you. But the anointing which you have received from Him abides in you, and you do not need that anyone teach you; but as the same anointing teaches you concerning all things, and is true, and is not a lie, and just as it has taught you, you will abide in Him." (1 John 2:24-27)

I, personally, had a fall from grace during my college years where I had succumbed to the darkness through my selfishness, arrogance, and alcohol abuse. It seemed as if there was a "God-shaped void" in my life, and I tried to fill that void with alcohol and mind altering substances, which was only helping me fall deeper into darkness. It took the hand of the Almighty to save me from that darkness. I am grateful to now be living in the light of His love. Some people live their entire lives in the darkness, full of contempt, hatred, and negative emotions, relying on man-made things to provide them happiness; that is truly unfortunate. Some people live their entire lives being both spiritually deaf and blind, never appreciating the true gift that is life. I can see this in people everywhere I go. I can see if a person is awake or asleep based on how he or she treats others, and the clarity of the eyes.

> "The lamp of the body is the eye. If therefore your eye is good, your whole body will be full of light. But if your eye is bad, your whole body will be full of darkness. If therefore the light that is in you is darkness, how great is that darkness!" (Matthew 6:22-23)

I can tell a person's relationship with God based upon how that person treats other people; whether or not he or she is helpful, kind, and nonjudgmental. I feel sorry for people who continually make excuses for themselves and have no idea how to be honest and truthful. I pray that you, dear reader, will find a way to figure this out during your life. I understand that there will be a day when I am held accountable for my actions, and I am judged according to my deeds and how I have judged others:

> "When the Son of Man comes in His glory, and all the holy angels with Him, then He will sit on the throne of His glory. All the nations will be gathered before Him, and He will separate them one from another, as a shepherd divides his sheep from the goats. And He will set the sheep on His right hand, but the goats on the left. Then the King will say to those on His right hand, "Come, you blessed of My Father, inherit the kingdom prepared for you from the foundation of the world: for I was hungry and you gave Me food; I was thirsty and you gave Me drink; I was a stranger and you took Me in; I was naked and you clothed Me; I was sick and you visited Me; I was in prison and you came to Me."
>
> Then the righteous will answer Him, saying, "Lord, when did we see You hungry and feed You, or thirsty and give You drink? When did we see You a stranger and take You in, or naked and

clothe You? Or when did we see You sick, or in prison, and come to You?" And the King will answer and say to them, "Assuredly, I say to you, inasmuch as you did it to one of the least of these My brethren, you did it to Me."

Then He will also say to those on the left hand, "Depart from Me, you cursed, into the everlasting fire prepared for the devil and his angels: for I was hungry and you gave Me no food; I was thirsty and you gave Me no drink; I was a stranger and you did not take Me in, naked and you did not clothe Me, sick and in prison and you did not visit Me."

Then they also will answer Him, saying, "Lord, when did we see You hungry or thirsty or a stranger or naked or sick or in prison, and did not minister to You?" Then He will answer them, saying, "Assuredly, I say to you, inasmuch as you did not do it to one of the least of these, you did not do it to Me." And these will go away into everlasting punishment, but the righteous into eternal life." (Matthew 25:31-46)

For He is not the God of the dead but of the living, for all live to Him. (Luke 20:38)

I am extremely grateful to have realized that in this life my actions do have consequences. I now understand that it is right to treat others with kindness, because God created all that is living. Having said that, I do my best to be skeptical because I also understand that some people are very evil and try to take advantage of others, however, I must not prejudge a person. In being awake spiritually, I now understand that in living honestly, truthfully, and away from the destructive ways of my past, my life has become heavenly; the kingdom of God is within me. The more love and kindness I show, the more I am blessed for it: "[God] Who has saved us and called us with a holy calling, not according to our works, but according to His own purpose and grace which was given to us in Christ Jesus before time began" (2 Timothy 1:9).

My life has been my own dream—not always perfect, but I know God has given me anything a person could ever hope for. I completely understand that if I were to have died two years ago in my car accident, I would have approached the pearly gates, stood before the Almighty, and it would have gone something like this: "Son of man, in whose name do you come before Me?" and I would have said, "Mikey B, sir," and He would have said, "I'm sorry, son; there's no 'Mikey B' on my list." On the contrary, if I were to die today and approach His Highness, it would go something like this: "Son of man, in whose name do you come before Me?" and I would say, "Well my Lord, my name is Michael. I understand that was the name that You chose for me, and You named me through my parents. When You gave me the gift of the spiritual awakening, I began to understand that Your way was much more enjoyable, peaceful, loving, and serene than my way. I did my best to live the *Way* You lived (a life of love, one precious moment at a time), I spoke the *Truth* (based on my life experiences and what You taught me) everywhere I went, and I thoroughly appreciated the gift that was my *Life*. At the age of twenty-six I came to understand that you had been living through me, with me, and in me the whole time. I tried to share the good news as best I could, and I hope that You find me worthy of Your Kingdom. I thank You so much for helping me to appreciate what a gift life really is. Thank You for teaching me how to live and how to love."

Closing

Well, that is what I have come to understand about God. God is a Spiritual being of emotions, creative intelligence, and will. God knows everything about me (He knows everything about you too, dear reader). I am grateful to now be living in His world, out of the darkness and into the light. I hope you enjoyed reading this as much as I enjoyed writing it for you. The truth is, I have been given an immense gift, and that is why I have written this book, for you dear reader. The free gift of an awakened soul is the most valuable thing I have ever received, and it is my job to share this free gift and how I have found it with you. I will say that I am not Jesus, and I am not "the Christ"; Jesus is, was, and always will be the Christ. My name is Michael, from the Hebrew for "Who Is Like God," and through God's grace, that is what I have become: a spiritual being clothed in the body of a man. The goal is to continue becoming more Christ-like. What I mean by this is that I need to be more loving, more forgiving, more compassionate, more understanding, more accepting, and less judgmental. I need to be rid of hatred, fear, guilt, resentment, and any form of bigotry or prejudice. I need to grow and become the person I was created to be. I am not perfect, and I am not the "Second Son of God" (I recently saw a young man on the Internet making that claim). "For false christs and false prophets will rise and show great signs and wonders to deceive, if possible, even the elect. See, I have told you beforehand" (Matthew 24:24-25).

Through spiritual growth and God's grace, I have become a child of the One True God, and the truth is, dear reader, you can too, if you seek Him sincerely through prayer and self-evaluation, and are willing to pursue an honest lifestyle. It is not about being "holier than thou";

it is about becoming a whole person (mind, body, and spirit). He is the Father, and we are His children, and now would be a good time to seek Him. "I love those who love me, and those who seek me diligently will find me" (Proverbs 8:17). From the apostle Paul: "And do this, knowing the time, that now it is high time to awake out of sleep; for now our salvation is nearer than when we first believed" (Romans 13:11).

Father, please let us awake from the spiritual sleep so that we no longer have to walk in darkness!

I shall leave you with some of my favorite pieces of Scripture:

"But the Helper, the Holy Spirit, whom the Father will send in My name, He will teach you all things, and bring to your remembrance all things that I said to you." (John 14:26)

But when the Helper comes, whom I shall send to you from the Father, the Spirit of truth who proceeds from the Father, He will testify of Me. (John 15:26)

Nevertheless I tell you the truth. It is to your advantage that I go away; for if I do not go away, the Helper will not come to you; but if I depart, I will send Him to you. And when He has come, He will convict the world of sin, and of righteousness, and of judgment: of sin, because they do not believe in Me; of righteousness, because I go to my Father and you see Me no more; of judgment, because the ruler of this world is judged.

I still have many things to say to you, but you cannot bear them now. However, when He, the Spirit of truth, has come, He will guide you into all truth; for He will not speak on His own authority, but whatever He hears He will speak; and He will tell you things to come. He will glorify Me, for He will take of what is Mine and declare it to you. All things that the Father has are

Mine. Therefore I said that He will take of Mine and declare it to you." (John 16:7-15)

My personal favorite:

"At that time Michael shall stand up, the great prince who stands watch over the sons of your people; and there shall be a time of trouble, such as never was since there was a nation, even to that time. And at that time your people shall be delivered, every one who is found written in the book. And many of those who sleep in the dust of the earth shall awake, some to everlasting life, some to shame and everlasting contempt. Those who are wise shall shine like the brightness of the firmament, and those who turn many to righteousness like the stars forever and ever. "But you, Daniel, shut up the words, and seal the book until the time of the end; many shall run to and fro, and knowledge shall increase." Then I, Daniel, looked; and there stood two others, one on this riverbank and the other on that riverbank." (Daniel 12:1-5)

Well, my name is Michael, and I am standing up under the grace of God and testifying with the Spirit of truth and my Lord Christ Jesus. It's funny, all the men of prophesy these days, but they failed to notice that Daniel saw two men. In my understanding, the first man was Jesus of Nazareth; time will tell who the second man is. I know that I cannot save the world, and I cannot give someone a spiritual awakening; however, I know there are many people looking for answers, and I know that having had these spiritual experiences in my life, and having gained a better understanding of the Creator, that it would have been a shame if I did not share these experiences with anyone who is willing to read. I understand that I have included quite a bit of Scripture; however, I find it most powerful when a living person speaks openly about his or her real-life spiritual experiences, because it is easier for a skeptic or someone seeking growth to understand the experiences and testimony of a living person than it is to hear someone just quoting from the Bible.

I can honestly say that without God I am nothing; at the very best I can only be two-thirds of a whole person without God—just a mind and a body without a soul—and I need God to be a whole person—mind, body, and spirit. If you are interested in experiencing how good life is with an awakened soul, the twelve steps is a great place to start, and all of the books I have referenced will help you grow in understanding. I pray, dear reader, that this book has helped you to better understand the Creator and how His world works. I shall finish by making you a promise. If you follow the twelve steps with an open heart and mind, it may not only save your life, but it may also save your soul. I hope this message reaches you with sincerity and in good faith, and until then I shall continue keeping the faith and standing up for the Father (or as I call Him: Abba, Adonai, and Yahweh) and His people. I shall continue walking in the light, and seeking to grow in oneness with my Creator, and living each day as if it were my last, until the time when He calls me back home to Him. May the grace, peace, love, and mercy of the Spirit of the living God be with you always. Amen.

Postscript

My journey of faith began with a simple belief in God. I mentioned how I felt the presence of His grace during the two-week program, so I knew He was real. In the beginning, my concept of God was: God, the Father; a God of love, peace, and forgiveness. Truthfully, dear reader, I had made many mistakes in my life, but it became very clear to me that He was willing to forgive me for my past mistakes. As I continued to grow, my concept of God grew to God Almighty, the Father of creation. I began to understand that He created me, and all he expected of me was to be an honest, kind, sober person. I also learned more about the Creator by listening to the experiences of other people, and how God had completely transformed their lives for the better. I understand that I may not always agree with another person, but I have no right to judge or harm that person, because God created him/her as well.

I continued to grow, and my perception became God: the Almighty Spirit of the universe, Creator of the heavens and the earth, and my Savior which is Christ the Lord. A deeper understanding, but I realized that I was learning to live the way He lived, speaking the truth based solely upon my experiences, and I had a newfound appreciation for my life. It took me about a month to accept Jesus Christ as my personal Savior. I suppose it could have been the skepticism of this world, or my own arrogance that was keeping me in the dark and out of the light, but I am very grateful that I woke up and accepted the free gift of eternal salvation. In my experience, God loves those who love Him, and He works with and for those who work for Him. The more I work for Him, the more He continues to fill me with His Spirit. I pray that you, dear reader, may experience the same.

I am not going to personally define my faith, because I see no need in labels; however, I accept Christ as my Savior and seek to follow Him; I accept His teachings and those of His apostles. I accept the teachings of Moses and the Ten-Commandments, and His true prophets. In abiding in the Ten Commandments, I know I shall not get into trouble with the laws of society, and it gives me inner purity and inner peace to do so. I will say that no person really has to define his faith, but all people really should try having some. In regards to the story of the footprints, I now thoroughly understand that during the pits and perils and dark hours of my life, the blackouts, and other low points, etc. those footprints are God's footprints, not mine. There are many times that I could have died, but I understand that it was His Spirit that was keeping me alive because He has a plan for me. He carried me through the difficult times and strengthened me, and I cannot express how grateful I am to have Him in my life.

It is a shame that in this day and age man has grown so out of touch with his spiritual nature that he questions the existence of his Creator. I sincerely hope that the ones who have denied His grace and gone as far as speaking out openly against God will be prepared to tell Him that when the time comes. In regards to science; I find science to be a great tool, and I am grateful for modern medicine since it has extended the lives of many loved ones. However science is certainly not the be-all and end-all, and I personally have a Bachelor of Science in Engineering from a very good school. No science can explain the spiritual experiences I have had, or the positive life changes I have undergone, and I have yet to find a science that will help me in everyday life situations including love, communication, and relationships.

About the Author

Author Michael Blomberg grew up in Groveland, Massachusetts. He is a graduate of Massachusetts Maritime Academy in Buzzards Bay, MA. Michael has been on a very in depth spiritual journey throughout most of his life, but in particular, since August, 2010. He has been touched by God's grace and wanted to share a positive truthful message with as many as who would read it, in hopes of giving people a better understanding of life.

Notes

Chapter 1: The Program

1. Don Miguel Ruiz, *The Four Agreements* (San Rafael, California: Amber-Allen Publishing, Inc., 1997).
2. David Jeremiah, *What in the World Is Going On?* (Nashville, Tennessee: Thomas Nelson, Inc., 2008).

Chapter 2: After the Program

1. *Twelve Steps and Twelve Traditions,* (Alcoholics Anonymous World Services, Inc., 1981).
2. Ruiz, *The Four Agreements.*
3. Kendra Noyes, "Salem man finds 2,000-year-old shekel on the shore." http://www.salemnews.com/local/x124780264/Salem-man-finds-2000-year-old-shekel-on-the-shore (accessed September 30, 2010).
4. *Alcoholics Anonymous World Services, Inc.,* fourth edition (New York: 2001), 63.
5. Rhonda Byrne, *The Secret,* (New York, NY: Atria Books, 2006).
6. Jeremiah, *What in the World Is Going On?*
7. Walvoord and Hitchcock, *Armageddon, Oil, and Terror* (Carol Stream, IL: Tyndale House Publishers, 2007), 65
8. Jonathan Sacks, *Future Tense* (New York: Schlocken Books, 2009).

9. *The Passion of the Christ*, DVD (Beverly Hills, California: ICON Productions, Twentieth Century Fox, 2004).

10. Beth Moore, *Paul 90 Days on His Journey of Faith* (Nashville, Tennessee: B&H Publishing Group, 2010), 299.

Chapter 3: Commandments, Golden Rule, Prayers, Finding the Narrow Way, God's Names

1. "Names of God." http://www.smilegodlovesyou.org/names.html.

Chapter 4: In Depth with the Spirit of the Universe

1. *Alcoholics Anonymous World Services, Inc.*, fourth edition (New York: 2001).

2. Peter Scholtes, "Holy Holy Holy (Hosanna)." http://www.worship.co.za/wsv/wsv-0604.asp.

3. Jeremiah, *What in the World Is Going On?*

Chapter 5: The End

1. *Alcoholics Anonymous World Services, Inc.*, fourth edition (New York, 2001), 13-14.

2. Mark Twain, "Concerning the Jews," *Harper's* (September 1899), 535.

3. *Forrest Gump*, videotape. (United States: Paramount Pictures, 1994).

4. *It's a Wonderful Life*, DVD. (Hollywood, California: Paramount Pictures, 1946).